INVISIBLE ILLNESS

Jake has taken on the bold task of being up front and honest about an issue that far too many of us struggle with, but don't know how to talk about. This book is a great resource for anyone who is dealing with anxiety, depression and any challenge of mental health. It is a powerful tool in learning how to receive God's grace for breakthrough while creating healthy habits and patterns that will lead to a life of victory.

Jared Ellis

Lead Pastor, E2 Church

Invisible Illness is a classic for this season! It's authentic, practical and easy to read so we can apply its principles to our everyday life!

Anthony Flores

Lead Pastor, Adventure Church

Jake Taylor is a man of passion, a man seeking truth and a man chasing after the heart of God. As a fellow sufferer of an anxiety disorder, I'm proud to partner with a man of this caliber in bringing these unique challenges to light. Jake is the real deal.

Lance Hahn

Senior Pastor, Bridgeway Christian Church

"We have had the privilege of knowing Jake Taylor since the day he was born. He has been like a nephew or a son to us, and even more than that because as he grew, he always had the heart and ability to serve others whenever needed. He is a gifted researcher, communicator, and gatherer, and the qualities we admire most about him are his authenticity, humility, and inclusiveness. This book could not have come at a better time, in a world that is drowning in isolation and an onslaught of warfare against the minds of people. Jake's story and personal revelations are sure to enlighten, educate, and encourage any reader, and we especially recommend this book to parents and pastors."

Don and Christa Proctor

President and Co-Director, City Pastors Fellowship

INVISIBLE ILLNESS

UNDERSTANDING AND THRIVING WITH ANXIETY AND DEPRESSION

By

JAKE TAYLOR

Invisible Illness: Understanding and Thriving with Anxiety and Depression

by Jake Taylor

© 2020 Jake Taylor

Unless otherwise indicated, Scripture quotations are taken from the Holy Bible, New Living Translation, copyright © 1996, 2004, 2007, 2013, 2015 by Tyndale House Foundation. Used by permission of Tyndale House Publishers, Inc., Carol Stream, Illinois 60188. All rights reserved.
Scripture quotations marked (NIV) are taken from the Holy Bible, New International Version®, NIV®. Copyright © 1973, 1978, 1984, 2011 by Biblica, Inc.® Used by permission of Zondervan. All rights reserved worldwide. www.zondervan.com The "NIV" and "New International Version" are trademarks registered in the United States Patent and Trademark Office by Biblica, Inc.®
Scripture marked ESV is taken from the ESV® Bible (The Holy Bible, English Standard Version®), copyright © 2001 by Crossway, a publishing ministry of Good News Publishers. Used by permission. All rights reserved."
Scripture marked KJV is taken from the Holy Bible, King James Version (Authorized Version).
Scripture marked VOICE is taken from The Voice™. Copyright © 2012 by Ecclesia Bible Society. Used by permission. All rights reserved.

Capitalization has occasionally been modified from the original.
Unless other noted, Greek and Hebrew translations are taken from Strong's Exhaustive Concordance of the Bible by James Strong, Copyright © 2009 by James Strong. Used by permission of Thomas Nelson. www.thomasnelson.com.

Cover by: Burconur
Interior Art by: Arian Mahusay

eBook ISBN: 978-1-7362813-1-4
Paperback ISBN: 978-1-7362813-0-7

ACKNOWLEDGEMENTS

I want to first thank Jesus, my King who rules over all the hardships that may come.

My wife, Rachel. You are my best friend, my boo thing, my rib. I love you so.

My son, Levi, I didn't know I could love like I love you. You've shown me a glimpse of the love of God.

My parents and siblings, I love you all. Thanks for the anecdotes and stories to make this book come alive.

My pastors, all of you. I love you all, thank you for being faithful and consistent.

The Father's House, the best church on the planet. Thank you for demonstrating what it means to be broken and messy but striving to look like Jesus more each day.

CONTENTS

FOREWORD

I used to think that successful pastors, entrepreneurs, and business leaders had it all together, thus enabling them to lead well and be successful. After pastoring and leading people for nearly 38 years, I am progressively and increasingly convinced that we are all just broken people on a broken planet trying to find our way to the healer. Some find him, and some give up, while others desperately search for him, not really knowing who it is they're looking for. But one thing remains a constant in our messed-up world; we all carry some measure of sickness, brokenness, and pain that only the Great Physician can heal. We are the clay on the wheel that is still in formation, the substance of a process, not the product of some event. Coming from a culture of the "quick fix" or "miracle moment", the author of this book takes you on a pain-filled and reality-based journey of walking with your brokenness while walking toward the light. He shares how you can deal with your pain while reaching for the healer and effectively live in the tension between where we are today and where God is calling us.

I'm convinced that arriving at the station of "being qualified" is an elusive target if not a myth. The idea that one day, in this life, we will be at a place spiritually, mentally, and emotionally where we can stand as the bonified experts and tell others how to "arrive" is an illusion, if not a deception. When we understand that brokenness, pain, inadequacy, and the ongoing internal struggle of insecurity and fear are part of the human experience, we can begin to move toward progressive healing and wholeness, thus accomplishing great things with our lives until the day of perfection comes. This book effectively calls us to recognize our anxiety, depression, pain, and brokenness to journey together toward progressive healing. We are called to great things; to give, love, serve, lead and grow - all while in need of healing from past wounds and hurts.

"Do it afraid." We are all familiar with this statement and the mentality it promotes. However, you can't afford to wait until you have fully overcome your fears to accomplish the things you are called to do, or you will never attempt anything. Take ground in life, win battles, start a business, perform in front of people, start a new relationship. Do it, afraid! I would submit that not only is the concept "do it afraid" reliable and proven advice, but the idea of "do it broken" is as valid and necessary. The author takes the time to research and unpack the varied levels of brokenness and pain that many people carry yet are afraid to address and talk about openly. The reality is that we all carry extra mental and emotional weight from the events of our lives, and we must be willing to identify and deal with it if we are to begin the journey to wholeness.

I genuinely believe that the following pages of this grace-packed book will help you find a greater degree of wholeness from anxiety and depression by helping you come closer to the healer. You will also experience a new level of love and compassion for those around you who are struggling with these same invisible foes. The impetus for the truth that comes from the following pages is not textbooks and a degree in psychology but from the life of a great leader in our church who has experienced the dark valley of depression and walked out the other side. This book comes from a heart that has been on a time-tested journey with Jesus and decided to continue to believe that what God has begun in his heart, He will be faithful to complete. I believe you will be significantly impacted and inspired by the chapters that lie ahead.

Dave Patterson

Lead Pastor, The Father's House

INTRODUCTION

The definition of *invisible* is simple—it means unable to be seen. You can have 20/20 vision and still not pick up on something invisible.

X-rays are invisible. But can be detected using special instruments.

Sound waves are invisible. But can deliver great beauty when heard.

Microwaves are invisible. Yet, when used in the correct context, provide great convenience for humanity.

Wind is invisible. Yet wind brings great force, and its effects are observable, even if we can't see the wind itself.

Many of us struggle with invisible illness. People you know, people you love, people you work with, people you bump into as you jaunt through your daily routines combat illnesses that are not easily observed with the naked eye. But the visibility or lack thereof of the illnesses does not render them powerless or fictitious.

I recently read through Jeremiah J. Johnston's book *Unanswered: Lasting Truth for Trending Questions*, which tackles "big questions" culture poses to Christian thinkers. Johnston has an entire section devoted to mental illness. He titles that section, "My Invisible Disease."[1] In it, he discusses the reality of mental illness and how the Western Church has historically addressed issues of mental illness and those inflicted. The real dilemma with mental illness is its invisibility. Without a trained eye, the correct questions, or proper engagement, you would never know someone was struggling.

Mental illness is invisible.

This book is simply a response from someone who has mental illnesses. As a disclosure, I am not a doctor or professional therapist. I am writing from the perspective of a Christian pastor who still has bouts of anxiety and depression.

Do I lack faith?

Am I living in serious unrepentant sin?

Am I living outside the will of God?

I don't think so; I do my best to repent quickly, invite accountability, and move in obedience. My aim is to be holy, as Jesus is holy. I fall woefully short, but I press on. All humans are in a process of becoming. Within that process is a struggle.

A fight.

A battle.

War wages on for the control of the direction of our lives, and some of our battles are fought in the context of the mind. My goal with this book is to implore us to slow down and observe. Maybe mental illness is something we should intentionally learn about. Maybe our battles as humans are unique to our individual journeys. Maybe it's best to take time to converse with one another rather than stereotyping and jumping to conclusions. Maybe even leaders struggle with invisible illnesses. And maybe that's okay.

PART ONE: ROOTS

CHAPTER 1

THE PROBLEM

> *Here is the test to find whether your mission on Earth is finished:*
> *If you're alive, it isn't.*
>
> *—Richard Bach*

I remember the day. Sleep eluded me, and my thoughts swirled around in my mind. I was unable to catch a single thought and force it to slow its pace. It seemed easier to command the wind to cease blowing or the waves to halt their crashing.

"You're worthless."
"You're alone."

"Your life has no value."
"End it."

Thought after thought cascaded through my mind with only negative conclusions presenting themselves as the correct course of action. *Why can't I slow my mind? Why can't I "take captive" these thoughts? Why can't I just "be positive?"*

I walked through crowds of familiar faces, all smiling, yet their greetings seemed hollow. Worthless. I was surrounded by crowds of "friends" while feeling completely and utterly alone. The grin painted across my face and the chorus of jokes that echoed from my lips gave the illusion that "I'm doing great! Couldn't be better if I tried!"

I was only eleven years old, and I wanted to kill myself.
I planned it.
I wanted it.

That night, I planned on putting an end to the misery that was my life. This was not the life I was promised. This was not "life and life more abundantly." Rather than taking my life, I settled for cutting myself, which somehow allowed the pain to leak out. I hurt myself, still alive but feeling dead.

As an eleven-year-old, I experienced what I had not yet learned verbiage for, the first of many battles I would wage with depression. As a young boy, all I knew was that what bombarded my mental space didn't match reality.

I was raised in an amazing family, with amazing parents and three younger siblings, which, while we are here, I would like to inform you makes me the alpha male. I may ever so frequently remind my siblings that I am the rightful heir to the birthright. My name, after all, is Jacob—I'll get it one way or another (cue corny Bible joke).

We were raised in church—pastors' kids from the jump. We attended church on Sunday mornings, Sunday nights, Tuesday-night prayer, Wednesday-night youth gatherings, and Thursday-night worship practice. On Friday nights, my parents taught some variation of a parenting class. It evolved through the years, but that schedule was fairly consistent. All that is to say, I had my fair share of church and, for the most part, I loved it. We did ministry as a family. We were a unit—the Taylor family—changing the world one church service at a time. Church people were my people—even the nasty hypocrites. I loved the whole lot of 'em. Until I was five years old.

There was a family that attended the church I grew up in that demonstrated a heart for broken, disenfranchised kids. They would frequently house between five and seven foster children at any given time. Little did anyone know, the "heart-for-broken-kids" masquerade was a front for sexual abuse in the shadows. Many children and teenagers came into their home broken and abused but, unfortunately, left even more broken and abused. For them, the label "Christian" would come to evoke horrific memories. One of those teenage boys, who had clearly been abused, graduated into sexually assaulting other young boys.

His first victim was five-year-old me.

Once my mind could comprehend what had been done to me, feelings of guilt, shame, and disillusionment became frequent companions. Part of eleven-year-old suicidal me, I believe, was correlated to five-year-old sexually abused me. Part of eleven-year-old suicidal me was linked to chemical imbalances in my brain. Part of eleven-year-old suicidal me was linked to generational inclinations toward anxiety and depression. We will discuss all of those factors, but I say this to say that invisible illnesses are complex, and many factors play into their manifestations.

A Widespread Problem

Mental illnesses have infected every sector of our society. Try as one may, no individual is immune to contracting and experiencing the many variations of mental illness. The National Alliance on Mental Illness reports one in five adults in America deals with some form of mental illness. Currently, ten million American adults experience what is described as a serious mental illness.[1] The NAMI breaks down these numbers by diagnosis:

- 1.1% (2.4 million) American adults live with schizophrenia
- 2.6% (6.1 million) American adults live with bipolar disorder
- 6.9% (16 million) American adults live with major depression
- 18.1% (42 million) American adults live with anxiety disorders

When adding up the statistics of diagnosed individuals, you end up with 66.5 million American adults living daily with mental illness. NAMI also estimates that a third of adults who suffer from various mental illnesses will never be diagnosed or seek treatment.[1]

Statistics across the board show that mental illnesses, especially depression and anxiety, are on the rise at alarming rates among children and adolescents. NBC found:

> The CDC says one in five children ages 3 through 17—about 15 million—have a diagnosable mental, emotional, or behavioral disorder in a given year. But only 20 percent of them get diagnosed or receive care.[2]

There is a problem with mental health in our country—a large segment of society struggles yet doesn't seem to feel it's vital to seek help. The question is, Why? Why don't those hurting get the help they need? Is it cost? Is it access to medical personnel and medicine? I believe cost and access play a role in individuals not seeking help for their mental well-being. But those structural issues are more difficult to diagnose, solve, and eradicate. Cost and access are subject to cultural and societal infrastructure. Changing those systems is a noble cause but not a simple one. I would propose there is another issue— an issue that we must take responsibility for, both within ourselves and in society. This issue is ingrained within our culture. Within our hearts. Within our beliefs and upbringings.

It is the stigma of mental health.

This is how Websters Dictionary defines *stigma*:

1. A mark of disgrace associated with a particular circumstance, quality, or person

A mark of disgrace. Mental illness has been seen as a mark of disgrace within society.

A sign of weakness.

A signal of frailty.

To this day, when I tell people that I struggle with depression and anxiety, I'm met with looks of shock, confusion, pity, and worry. A look of *I don't know how to respond* is plastered all over their faces. Throw into the mix that I am a pastor, and now people are really thrown for a loop. Sometimes, I like to poke the bear a bit and reveal that I take medication for my conditions. The words that follow are often comedic, to say the least.

"God heals, you know?"
"Oh, that's nice…"
"Have you prayed about that?"

No Karen, I haven't prayed about it. I enjoy the gnawing sense of hopelessness. I don't really say that, but I want to sometimes.

Thankfully, studies from The Barna Group show that younger generations are more accepting of mental illness and seeking out treatment.[3] When speaking generally, approval of counseling, medication, and treatment for mental illness varies depending on the age demographic. The same studies show that "4 in 10 American adults (42 %) have seen a counselor."

It goes on to state:

> By all measures, Millennials and Gen X have more interest in counseling than Boomers and Elders. One-fifth of Millennials (21 %) and 16 percent of Gen X are currently engaged in therapy. By comparison, only 8 percent of Boomers and 1 percent of Elders are presently working with a counselor or therapist.... Just 15 percent of Millennials and 18 percent of Gen X say they never would go to counseling, 30 percent of Boomers and 34 percent of Elders feel this way.

Different age demographics have very different approaches to mental health and how it should be treated. One generation is berating the other to "man up", to "stop being snowflakes", while the other is unwilling to honor and respect those who have gone before them and learn a lesson or two from experience and wisdom. Neither approach is constructive. In the crossfire are casualties consisting of people who largely didn't ask for the hand they have been dealt. Nevertheless, they have to figure out how to manage the load they carry. Individuals are wounded as culture and society subscribe to an unhealthy stigma around mental health.

Church-World Stigmas

In the Church world, the stigma is worse. Those who deal with varying mental ailments are often labeled as faithless, sinful, not committed, and ultimately useless for ministry.

Growing up, I was often disillusioned and disappointed hearing pastors speak of having overcome obstacles in the past yet never mentioning problems that they were currently facing. They would speak of the pride of yesterday or the addiction of times past, but there was an illusion of grandeur surrounding the present. These pastors would often reflect an aura of perfection and complete certainty.

"You too can be where I am one day."

"Pray harder; do more; have more faith, and it will all go away."

"The best is yet to come. In fact, the best is my NOW."

Doubts never surfaced. Sorrow was fleeting. This seemed unattainable. Undoable. Unreachable. Can anyone live in such an ivory tower of confidence?

I come from a charismatic tradition, and I believe all the gifts of the Spirit are for today, for the believer, and for the edification of the Church. I disclose that to say I believe that in an instant, God can heal mental illness. I've seen it happen on dozens of occasions. I've seen things that logic and reason cannot explain. He is a creative God, who still performs creative miracles. But I have had dozens of people pray for me, with me, and about me for the afflictions I carry. Yet, to this day, I have not been healed. I still deal with depression and anxiety on a regular basis.

I love Jesus.
I love the Church.
I tithe.
I have faith.
I'm as faithful as I know how to be in pastoring people.

The Example of Jesus

In John 8, Jesus is with His disciples in Jerusalem. He has just finished a sparring match with the religious leaders of the day. Shortly after, He issues one of the most encouraging, hopeful declarations in Christendom:

> So if the Son sets you free, you are truly free. (John 8:36 NLT)

He continues to walk along with His disciples, when they notice a man who was born blind. Cause and effect were common thought in antiquity. Clearly, sin causes physical brokenness. The disciples assumed the misery this man endures is due to his own sinfulness or perhaps the sin of his parents. The IVP New Testament Commentary comments on this passage, stating:

> People commonly assumed that disease and disorders on both the personal and national level were due to sin, as summarized in the rabbinic saying from around A.D. 300 that "there is no death

without sin and there is no suffering without iniquity" (b. Shabbat 55a). But the case of a person born blind raises the question of whose sin caused this condition, that of his parents or of the person himself while in the womb.[4]

First-century Jews would often quote Exodus 20:5 when clinging to causality.

> For I, the LORD your God, am a jealous God, punishing the children for the sin of the parents to the third and fourth generation of those who hate Me.

The disciples offer Jesus two options when attributing blame for the blindness: the parent's sin or the man's sin. One of them is guilty. Jesus's response is counterculture.

> "Neither this man nor his parents sinned," said Jesus, "but this happened so that the works of God might be displayed in him." (John 9:3)

Jesus institutes an important theological principle for twenty-first-century disciples today—bad things happen to everyone. Yes, the law of reciprocity is still alive and well, but we are confined to a fallen, sinful world where bad things do happen to good people. Jesus states in the Sermon on the Mount, "He causes His sun to rise on the evil and the good and sends rain on the righteous and the unrighteous" (Matthew 5:45).

MATTHEW 5:45 NIV

"HE CAUSES HIS SUN TO RISE
ON THE EVIL AND THE GOOD,
AND SENDS RAIN ON THE
RIGHTEOUS AND THE
UNRIGHTEOUS."

Bad things happen to bad people, and bad things happen to good people. Good things happen to good people, and good things happen to bad people. Again, earth is a fallen, broken planet, and the utopia we were designed to experience has been marred by sin. Disease, sickness, and, yes, even invisible illnesses happen to good and bad people alike. Mental illness is a struggle for many who have submitted their lives to the Lordship of Jesus. We attach undue shame, guilt, and rejection to people when we do not reject the stigmas attached to mental illness.

For a moment, let's specifically talk about the Church world. We need to intentionally destroy within our places of worship the stigma that comes with mental illness. The culture and stigmas that are present within our churches are there either because of purposeful intent or from allowing toxic behaviors to linger. Both require intentionality. You are either intentionally creating a culture of honesty or intentionally allowing a toxic stigma to remain. Speak to invisible illness with consistency, and shatter unhealthy stigmas. We must create space for healing to occur.

The Barna Group reports that only 4 percent of individuals who seek counseling do so because a pastor advised them to.[5] One factor Barna refers to is "a pastor's reticence in recommending counseling." The same study indicates that one in three non-Christians (33 percent) seeks treatment for mental illness, which is over twice the percentage (15 percent) among Christians.

Non-Christians are over twice as likely as Christians to get the help they need for a very real illness. If you are a pastor reading this, take this to heart. For your people, for your family, for the love of God—remove the stigma from mental health and push your people toward wholeness.

Deep Dark Secret

As a pastor, I am in a unique place to speak on some of the pressures pastors and leaders experience. For a moment, let me speak to pastors and those in high-level leadership. The role of a pastor is unlike any other. The people pastors serve expect them to be the CEO, counselor, wedding officiant, funeral preacher, event planner, team builder, money guru, budget constructer, world-class speaker, and worship leader, while also being present for every event. But don't forget, they must also be at every one of their own kids' ball games, maintain a date night with their wives, and be the priest of their homes. If you can do all of this simultaneously, you'll be a great pastor. However, there is a problem.

That. is. impossible.

Every decision you make is second-guessed. You can't please everyone—haters are in the ranks. Without intentionality, mental well-being goes by the wayside.

Anyone who has ever pastored knows that there are questions people ask whose answers vary depending on who the asker is. We have canned responses for different kinds of askers.

Here is a sample question:

"How are you, Pastor?"

Doesn't seem complicated. Seems straightforward enough, right? Or so you would think—but it isn't. If you are a pastor or a high-level leader, you know the answer to that question depends on who is asking it.

Recently, I was having a conversation with a pastor friend of mine. He is one of those friends that I can be real with. We can ugly cry, snot bubbles and all. We were discussing this very topic. With disappointment in his eyes, he stated that many people ask that question but don't really want to know the answer. Our culture has conditioned us to believe pastors are to be strong men and women of valor with few-to-no struggles. At the first sign of weakness, usability for ministry can be brought into question. This conditioning has bred guarded pastors, who keep their cards close to their chests with people, one another, their loved ones, and even with God. So, our canned responses spill out:

"Blessed and highly favored!"
"Anointed and appointed!"
"SO great!"

When reality may be:

"I'm depressed and feel hopeless."
"I'm anxious and can't keep a single thought straight."
"I can't measure up to expectations, and I've had real thoughts of taking my own life."

Those examples would have been some of my real answers in certain seasons of my life. Without being intentional in nurturing mental health, we don't stand a chance of making it over the long haul. We can't live up to unrealistic expectations, and we can't allow those expectations to drive us to a place of ruin. But, unfortunately, for many of us, the pressure has driven us to a place of mental exhaustion.

These unique pressures lead to unique experiences that can result in mental illnesses. Many leaders, including pastors, have a deep, dark secret that they feel must stay hidden. That secret is their invisible illness. There is a good chance you as a leader, or the person you follow, is dealing with or has dealt with some form of mental illness during their tenure. With leadership comes pressure, and with pressure often comes depression and anxiety.

Influence Magazine published an article that found 46 percent of pastors state they have dealt with depression while pastoring. Sixty-two percent of pastors of smaller, struggling churches have experienced depression.[6] This is not just "the people's" issue; this is something many leaders face.

Maybe it's time we stop trying to be Superman and instead, opt to lead from our weakness. Could it be that God really is glorified in our weakness?

Could it be that God desires for you to take off the "I'm-doing-great" mask and lead from a place of vulnerability? Perfection is not possible; that isn't the example we see in Scripture.

Thorn in the Flesh

Paul famously had a "thorn in the flesh." God apparently doesn't feel it's necessary to tell us what that thorn in the flesh was. There are many theories out there—many believe it had something to do with his eyesight, but no one really knows. One thing is certain—this thorn in the flesh was a nuisance to Paul. He states in 2 Corinthians 12:7b–10:

> In order to keep me from becoming conceited, I was given a thorn in my flesh, a messenger of Satan, to torment me. Three times I pleaded with the Lord to take it away from me. But He said to me, "My grace is sufficient for you, for My power is made perfect in weakness." Therefore I will boast all the more gladly about my weaknesses, so that Christ's power may rest on me. That is why, for Christ's sake, I delight in weaknesses, in insults, in hardships, in persecutions, in difficulties. For when I am weak, then I am strong.

Paul was tormented by this thorn and pleaded with God to remove it. God, in His omniscience, denied Paul's request. For many of us, this would be a point of contention that would result in bitterness and disillusionment. Many of us would begin to hide the thorn, deny the thorn, and pretend we've overcome the thorn. But what if God calls you and me to *embrace* the thorn?

Let's go back for a moment to Jesus and the disciples discussing the man born blind. Jesus remarks that the blindness is there to display the power of God. The man's weakness can be used to reflect God's omnipotence. Could it be that your thorn is there to reveal the power of God? The man born blind is miraculously healed, and all the onlookers are drawn to the beauty and supremacy of Jesus. Paul says that he not only began to embrace the thorn, but he boasted about it! It's as if Paul were exclaiming:

"God is ALLOWING me to be weak so that He can manifest His strength THROUGH my life."

What if the invisible illness you and I face is not us being disciplined, ignored, or abused by God? What if the invisible illness we carry is a method through which the power of God is shown? Maybe God is allowing your suffering to enable empathy within you for a people group you would have otherwise overlooked. God uses all things—maybe your thorn is designed to be a platform for ministry.

The Prince of Preachers

Charles Spurgeon is known as the "Prince of Preachers." He is credited with writing over 140 books, publishing and editing his sermons every Sunday, responding to hundreds of letters weekly, founding the Metropolitan Tabernacle Pastor's College, and pastoring a large church called New Park Street Chapel. Spurgeon was undoubtedly one of the most influential pastors and theologians of the nineteenth century. On October 19, 1856, at the ripe young age of twenty-two, Charles Spurgeon stood up to preach at the Music Hall of the Royal

Surrey Gardens. It is estimated that a crowd of over seven thousand gathered to hear the Word proclaimed. During the event, one attendee yelled Fire! The masses began to stampede as they ran for safety. The result was devastating—seven dead and twenty-eight injured.

His wife records that Spurgeon was forever impacted by that fateful event.

> My beloved's anguish was so deep and violent, that reason seemed to totter in her throne, and we sometimes feared that he would never preach again.[7]

Spurgeon suffered from severe depression the rest of his earthy life. He would often speak of the anguish in his soul, as he pastored his church and sought to raise up other pastors. He is quoted as saying:

> I could say with Job, "My soul chooseth strangling rather than life." I could readily enough have laid violent hands upon myself, to escape from my misery of spirit.[8]

As a pastor first, Spurgeon used these experiences to relate to those who were afflicted with a tormented mind. He used his depression to learn from God and relate to those who bore His image. He found the good even in his brokenness. He stated:

> It is good for a man to bear the yoke; good for a man to breast the billows; good for a man to pass

through fire and through water, and so to learn sublime lessons.[9]

He did not demonize the invisible illness he experienced; he used it as a tool to connect with people.

A. W. Tozer says this:

> We tend to think of Christianity as a painless system by which we can escape the penalty of past sins and attain to heaven at last. The flaming desire to be rid of every unholy thing and to put on the likeness of Christ at any cost is not often found among us. We expect to enter the everlasting kingdom of our Father and to sit down around the table with sages, saints, and martyrs; and through the grace of God, maybe we shall; yes, maybe we shall. But for the most of us, it could prove at first an embarrassing experience. Ours might be the silence of the untried soldier in the presence of the battle-hardened heroes who have fought the fight and won the victory and who have scars to prove that they were present when the battle was joined.
>
> The devil, things, and people being what they are, it is necessary for God to use the hammer, the file, and the furnace in His holy work of preparing a saint for true sainthood. *It is doubtful whether God can bless a man greatly until He has hurt him deeply.*[10]

I believe God heals, delivers, and restores, but I also know He allows suffering to refine us and conform us into the image of Christ. My pastor, Dave Patterson, says it best: "We pray until." We pray for God to heal; we pray for God to restore; we believe for a miracle, but even in the face of what may appear like unanswered prayers, we are to declare, "When I am weak, then I am strong," because HIS power is made perfect in weakness.

Maybe it's not shameful for pastors, leaders, and everyone in between to deal with mental illness. We need to embrace our thorns and boast in our weakness, as we watch the strength of God reveal itself in our lives.

CHAPTER 2

HURTS SO GOOD

A pastor's work is an anxious one.

—Charles Spurgeon

Some reading this book may never have experienced an invisible illness. Maybe the concept of depression or anxiety is hard to grasp. I want to use this chapter to frame what some of those illnesses feel like. I'm going to lay out what my experience is, what some of my friends' experiences have been, and what some characters in the Bible experienced.

And, yes, Biblical characters dealt with these issues too.

My First Issue: Depression

As stated in the previous chapter, I've dealt with depression for most of my life. Depression has revealed its ugly face more times than I care to count. I have already recounted the first time depression introduced itself. I wish that were the only time I've experienced this particular illness, but it isn't.

For our purposes here, I want to detail a few of my darker moments in order to explain what a depressive episode may feel like. Understanding and seeking to understand is hugely important.

At sixteen, I was the typical popular teenage boy you see on every high-school TV show. Basically, my life was *High School Musical*. I'll pretend I was Zac Efron—it's good for my self-esteem. I played football; I was dating a cheerleader; I had all the friends you think a hormonal kid would need to have. My brother and I were in and out of bands that had a fair amount of notoriety, and we played on stages with national acts. Hundreds of people came to our shows, singing lyrics back to us that we had written in our bedrooms. Through my high-school years, I would be a rally commissioner, student-body vice president, drumline captain, and homecoming king. I was at or was throwing every party—and yet, I was horribly, deeply depressed. I coped with my mental illness with alcohol, promiscuity, and porn addiction.

Even with all the accolades, I never felt like I was enough. It was as if I expected rejection to show up any minute. This state of acceptance felt fragile. Abandonment would catch me by surprise. I've always been a glass-half-full person, but I was waiting for someone to invade my life of bliss and shatter any optimism that lingered. My mind was unable to be positive. Positive thinking didn't seem to be within my scope.

One night in particular, I did as most sixteen-year-old boys do—I argued with my parents. For whatever reason, in my mind, this argument was too much to handle. My sick mind interpreted an argument as rejection. Rejection was unfathomable. Unacceptable. Unlivable. I penned a suicide note and went to take my last shower before ending my life. I returned to my room to find my mom tearfully reading the note. Her response put a halt to my plans that night.

Depression is mentally debilitating. When someone is truly depressed, being positive feels as easy as deadlifting a car. It's a daunting challenge. Joy feels fleeting, happiness a distant memory. Regardless of what life looks like from the outside in, it feels hopeless from the inside out.

It's an illness.

It's a sickness.

Illnesses aren't reasoned away. They must be treated.

I was an intern at a church right out of high school for two years. The joy of my life was serving young folks and watching them experience the love of God. There is an adrenaline rush in watching the proverbial light flip on in someone's soul as they encounter the extravagant love of the Creator. "*THAT God loves me?*" I live for it.

During the second year of my internship, good ol' depression came back with a vengeance. One day, with the rest of the second-year interns, gathered around a table at Nugget Market, BLTs in hand, I confessed what was going on in my mind. I'll never forget one of the responses I received after I had poured out my soul and allowed my weakness to be laid bare. The response was:

"Why are you so sad?"

He didn't get it.

Why am I so sad?

Sadness is not what this is.

Sadness and depression are not the same things. Sadness can be reasoned with. Your kid is sad when they don't get Skittles. Being out of your favorite coffee makes you sad. Your team losing a game makes you sad. Untreated depression makes you want to kill yourself.

Depression can feel like your head is being crushed like a grape. Thoughts swirl. Desire is lost. Taste loses its potency. Things that once satisfied feel foolish. That's depression.

After my internship, I became a youth pastor, taking over from my parents. The transition was smooth, and the ministry was, by every metric, a success. Every week, students were submitting their lives to the Lordship of Christ. Numerically, we were growing. The culture of our youth ministry was amazing. It was fun, it was life giving, it was a party. There was only one problem: I was massively depressed and so was my wife.

In this season, depression manifested itself in a new way. There were days when I would lie in bed from eight AM to eight PM, unable to move, calling in sick to work. Those calls are hard. It's hard to call in sick for mental illness. It's hard to explain to someone else that your mind is making it impossible to function. It's difficult to explain that you don't know why you are completely shutting down.

Depression steals the simple joys of life. I had no sex drive—no desire for intimacy. My temper was short. I lost all motivation, all interest, and all ability to function as a human. All creativity was gone. My wife and I isolated ourselves from everyone we loved and cared for. We wanted to reach out for help but felt unable to summon up the courage to invite in backup.

I remember a particular day I lay in bed for ten hours, and my wife lay on the kitchen floor for the same stint. Both unable to function. This all transpired while in ministry, loving people, loving Jesus, and leading a successful ministry.

Everyone's encounter with the invisible illness of depression is different. However, depression is not about being sad. It's not a fancy way of saying "bummed out." It's a debilitating illness with massive consequences. Some of you may relate to these struggles; others may be learning about them for the first time. If you are in the midst of a battle, here is my tip:

GOD NEVER WASTES PAIN

It can get better if you treat it. Don't suffer alone.

Fight through apathy and invite others into your pain.

God *never* wastes pain.

If you are being educated on the realities of depression, use this opportunity to correctly love those who suffer. Those who suffer from chronic depression often want to reach out for help but physically can't seem to do it. There were times I wanted to scream for help, but I couldn't muster the physical strength to ask for it. I want to encourage you to be proactive—don't allow friends to isolate and suffer alone. Depression mutes the hurting, depletes strength from the strong, and perpetuates hopelessness.

My Second Issue: Anxiety

One invisible illness isn't enough, so in the wise, timeless words of the prophet D. J. Khaled:

"Anotha one!"

Let's talk about anxiety. Until the last few years, I wouldn't have said anxiety was an issue of mine, because I didn't have the verbiage to express what I have felt for years.

As of the time of writing this book, my wife and I have been campus pastors for three years. We are a part of a multi-site church that is growing and thriving. We have the tremendous opportunity to pastor some of the most amazing people on the planet. I've always been a people person, and I get tremendous joy in welcoming first-time guests. I'm familiar with the sting of rejection and have an "allergy" to people being isolated. The church should be the most welcoming, inviting, warm entity on planet earth. I *LOVE* creating that atmosphere.

A year and a half into our tenure, seemingly out of nowhere, the thought of interacting with crowds brought on debilitating fear followed by hyperventilating on Sunday mornings. I would get the most intense, painful feeling of nervousness, followed by the inability to breathe or stay standing. I found myself hiding in a bathroom prior to each service, practicing breathing techniques in an attempt to avoid blacking out. I forced myself to exit the bathroom and welcome the people I was called to pastor, the whole time mentally freaking out.

There were times when I had to speak, but I couldn't get a single thought straight in my mind. I would be walking up the stairs of the stage thinking to myself, *I can't remember a single concept in this message I have to preach.* Then boom—game time. Sink or swim.

That was the first time I encountered social anxiety. This would continue for over a year, before I did anything to treat what was going on in my mind. Concentration feels impossible in the middle of an anxiety attack.

My wife was the one who shed light on what my experience was called.

Healthline outlines eleven signs and symptoms of anxiety disorders:

1. Excessive worrying

2. Feeling agitated
3. Restlessness
4. Fatigue
5. Difficulty concentrating
6. Irritability
7. Tense muscles
8. Trouble falling or staying asleep
9. Panic attacks
10. Avoiding social situations
11. Irrational fears[1]

I deal with eleven out of eleven. Do I win anything? Is there a prize? I'd like a red gumball, please. Anxiety is unique, because it can simultaneously attack your mind and your body. You can feel like an invisible giant is strangling you, while worrying about paying the mortgage, while having an irrational fear of solar flares, all the while being unable to concentrate on a single topic. Anxiety and panic go hand in hand.

In his book, *How to Live in Fear*, Pastor Lance Hahn details his experience with a panic disorder. In the second chapter, he outlines what adulthood looks like from the perspective and experience of someone who has battled panic and anxiety disorders. He details an encounter he once had just prior to stepping on stage to preach.

> My chest started to tighten. I hadn't been able to get a deep breath all morning, but now it was getting worse. Fatigue washed over me in waves, and now the fight-or-flight symptoms of my panic

disorder began to overtake me. In a daze, I forced myself to go into the sanctuary, as I prepared to walk on to the stage, I felt my legs go numb. I was going to collapse. I told my assistant to get the band ready to do another worship set if I couldn't continue. I also asked her to get another pastor on standby to jump in, in case I couldn't finish. As she dashed off, the announcement videos were winding down. I forced myself up the stairs and clutched the lectern. As the lights came up, and one thousand pairs of eyes locked on me, I was fully exposed with no place to run.

What should I do?[2]

Lance outlines a singular moment of panic and anxiety. One moment.

These episodes are common with those who struggle with various invisible illnesses.

The Bible and Invisible Illness

The Bible may rarely use the word *depression* and never utilize the phrase *mental illness*, but by examining the lives of people in Scripture, we can determine that some dealt with the same things we do. Let's briefly look at a few characters who demonstrated invisible illness.

Elijah

Elijah is undoubtedly one of the most heroic characters in the Old Testament. Only two Biblical characters did not see death: Enoch and Elijah. Elijah's name means "Yahweh is my God." He first appears in 1 Kings 17, pronouncing an end of rain until he says so. This decree goes to none other than the infamous king of Israel, King Ahab. Safe to say, he starts with a bang. He continues on to the city of Zarephath, where a miracle of provision for a widow and her son takes place. That son dies, and Elijah raises him back to life. Then comes one of the most heralded moments in the Old Testament: the pray-off.

Chapter 18 begins with God telling Elijah to head back to King Ahab and announce an imminent end to the three-year drought. Elijah appears before Ahab, and a challenge ensues.

> "Now summon all Israel to join me at Mount Carmel, along with the 450 prophets of Baal and the 400 prophets of Asherah who are supported by Jezebel." ... Then Elijah said to them, "I am the only prophet of the LORD who is left, but Baal has 450 prophets. Now bring two bulls. The prophets of Baal may choose whichever one they wish and cut it into pieces and lay it on the wood of their altar, but without setting fire to it. I will prepare the other bull and lay it on the wood on the altar, but not set fire to it. Then call on the name of your god, and I will call on the name of the LORD. The god who answers

by setting fire to the wood is the true God!" And all the people agreed. (1 Kings 18:19, 22–24 NLT)

So, we have Elijah, the Man of God, vs. Ahab, the ungodly, wicked king, his four hundred and fifty prophets of Baal, and four hundred prophets of Asherah engaged in a pray-off. Whoever's prayer God answers by fire wins.

The pagan prophets begin their ritualistic dances, expending every last bit of energy to summon their god. They cut themselves, hoping their blood will cry out and persuade Baal to intervene. Silence. No god is answering. Elijah, channeling his inner *Jersey Shore* in a truly petty manner, begins to mock the priests. He suggests that maybe their god had to use the restroom, or maybe he's on vacation. His retorts only fuel the priests' pleas. Again, silence. No response from their pagan gods.

Elijah then begins to rebuild the altar of the Lord, using twelve stones, one for each tribe of Israel. He digs a broad trench around the altar and lays the wood, along with the sacrifice, upon the altar. What comes next is something that makes no logical sense. He drenches the sacrifice with water. Not once, not twice, but three times. The sacrifice is soaked, the trench overflowing, the altar dripping with water—which, by the way, isn't exactly conducive to fire. Then Elijah prays.

Instantly, fire consumes the sacrifice, the altar, and all the water. Yahweh answers by fire. The people respond in awe, and they fall face down and begin to worship. Elijah responds by killing all the pagan prophets.

However, Elijah isn't done being used by God for miracles that day. He climbs up Mount Carmel and prays seven times that rain will come. Keep in mind it has not rained in three years. He presses through six unanswered prayers until the seventh proves fruitful. Soon, the clouds turn to black, and a terrific rainstorm ensues.

Fire from heaven, rain restored. Elijah the Man of Faith. The Man of God.

But after these great victories come great threats. Queen Jezebel is not pleased with Elijah slaying her prophets. In fact, Scripture records she tells Elijah, "May the gods strike me and even kill me if by this time tomorrow I have not killed you just as you killed them" (1 Kings 19:2 NLT). Fear sets into the heart of Elijah, and he flees for his life. Leaving his servant behind, he sets out into the wildness. Alone and afraid. This man of victory is now reduced to a loner in the wilderness. This is where depression sets in. Listen for yourself.

> Then he went on alone into the wilderness, traveling all day. He sat down under a solitary broom tree and prayed that he might die. "I have had enough, LORD," he said. "Take my life, for I am no better than my ancestors who have already died." (1 Kings 19:4 NLT)

Elijah goes from the victorious pray-off champion to wishing God would kill him.

James states in his letter that, "Elijah was a man just like us" (James 5:17 BSB). Most of the time when that verse is quoted, people only grab hold of the superhuman connection Elijah seemingly had with Almighty God. Rightfully so, I might add. The context in that verse is the power of prayer. However, Elijah was a man like you, like me. He struggled, he had victories, and he had defeats. Highs and lows. Mountaintops and valleys. He was a man, just like me, just like you. He dealt with the same human emotions we do. On the heels of supernatural victory, Elijah experienced emotional defeat. A man just like us.

Sunday afternoons and evenings are vulnerable times for me. Our Sunday morning services are usually marked with the tangible presence of God and people surrendering their lives to Jesus. It fires me up. Yet, hours later, I often find myself depressed or anxious. The high of triumph oftentimes is followed by a valley of despair. It's a weird phenomenon. Frequently, when I discuss these happenings with those who suffer from an invisible illness, I find that I am not alone. Elijah, Man of God, Man of Victory, also depressed, pleading with God to end his life.

David

David is probably the most prominent, Scripture-rich character we have in the Bible who clearly deals with waves of invisible illness. David, the shepherd boy anointed king, slays literal giants and also giants of the mind. Let's do a quick survey of his life. He is the youngest of eight sons, the runt of the litter. One day, the prophet/priest-turned-judge Samuel heads into town to anoint the next king of Israel. God is rejecting Saul, and the mantle of leadership of the nation will be passed on. God tells Samuel that the next king will be a son of Jesse. So, Samuel marches up to Jesse's house and tells Jesse to bring in all his sons. Somehow, Jesse doesn't bother to bring in David.

Surely, David couldn't be the one the Lord would choose.

David is the young, scrawny, emotional kid who hangs with and sings to the sheep all day. Not exactly Daddy's favorite kid. But God chooses him. Samuel anoints David, and Scripture records that "the Spirit of the LORD came powerfully upon David from that day on" (1 Samuel 16:13).

Meanwhile, the Spirit of the Lord leaves King Saul, and a spirit is sent to torment him. Relief only comes when the young shepherd boy, David, plays the harp. Saul loves David and recruits him to bear his armor.

One day, while in between the pastures of his father's home, Jesse summons David and tasks him with delivering food to his brothers, who are at war. Israel is at war with the Philistines, and their champion, Goliath of Gath, threatens the nation of Israel, while the Israelite army cowers in fear. While delivering groceries, David hears the threats and decides to act. In fact, he offers to fight the giant and, after some convincing, he stands toe to toe with his foe. The shepherd vs. the man of war.

A battle for freedom. We all know how this iconic story ends—the shepherd boy is victorious, and the Israelites prevail over their nemesis.

David's fame begins to spread throughout the region. Even servant girls pen songs that exalt this shepherd boy over the king, which rubs the king the wrong way. Saul won't have this. No mere shepherd boy will absorb the fame due the king. The same king who once adored the shepherd-turned-musician-turned-giant killer now begins to throw spears. David is forced to flee.

For the next decade-plus, David spends his every waking minute avoiding sure death at the hands of this mad king. He hides in forests, caves, mountains, cities, valleys, the wilderness, and foreign nations, all for the sin of being anointed and chosen by God. During this season of exile, we find the most beautiful psalms composed by David, as he pours his heart out with complete abandon. We see the contents of his heart, his mind, and his soul. Though he is quick to honor God, it does not negate the pain within his mind. Here is an example, where we observe David speaking of his condition:

> Have compassion on me, LORD, for I am weak.
> Heal me, LORD, for my bones are in agony.
> I am sick at heart.
> How long, O LORD, until You restore me?...
> I am worn out from sobbing.
> All night I flood my bed with weeping,
> drenching it with my tears.

My vision is blurred by grief;
my eyes are worn out because of all my enemies.
(Psalm 6:2–3, 6–7 NLT)

If that doesn't sound like depression, I don't know what does. David pours out his heart to God in the psalms; they are rich and robust. They are soaked in authenticity and lament. Read through them.

Another psalm that lends itself to vulnerability is Psalm 42. Psalm 42 is believed to have been written by David and performed by the sons of Korah, composed either as David evaded Saul or fled for his life from Absalom. Spurgeon states:

> That choice band of singers, the sons of Korah, are bidden to make this delightful Psalm one of their peculiars…. Although David is not mentioned as the author, this Psalm must be the offspring of his pen; it is so Davidic, it smells of the son of Jesse, it bears the marks of his style and experience in every letter. We could sooner doubt the authorship of the second part of Pilgrim's Progress than question David's title to be the composer of this Psalm.[3]

Listen to the son of Jesse, as he allows his anguish to gush onto the paper.

As the deer longs for streams of water,
so I long for You, O God.
I thirst for God, the living God.

When can I go and stand before Him?
Day and night I have only tears for food,
while my enemies continually taunt me, saying,
"Where is this God of yours?"
My heart is breaking
as I remember how it used to be.
(Psalm 42:1–4 NLT)

David is in agony of mind and soul, remembering what once was. He wears his heart on his sleeve, whether it be full of hope or clinging to the promises of God. Yet, even in the midst of pain and suffering, he chooses to direct his meditation to the goodness of God. In these psalms, you find a constant theme of lament and then a turning of the soul toward the faithfulness of Yahweh. Psalm 42 concludes with David declaring this:

Why am I discouraged?
Why is my heart so sad?
I will put my hope in God!
I will praise Him again—
my Savior and my God!
(Psalm 42:11 NLT)

He chooses in the midst of agony to direct his adoration to God. To link his hope to God. To set his heart/mind/soul on the promises of God.

We can learn from his reflection in the midst of the dark night of the soul. Where are we directing the reflection of our hearts and minds? Many heroes of our faith dealt with invisible illnesses. I have mentioned two of many broken vessels used by the Potter. Find rest and comfort in the company you are surrounded by. Invisible illnesses are common to humanity.

Empathy

Empathy is defined as the ability to understand and share the feelings of another.

The mistake many followers of Jesus make is believing God has called us to sympathy. *Sympathy* means feeling bad for the plight of another. God is not a God of sympathy; He invaded human history to encounter and experience what it means to be human, not just to feel bad for us from a distance. The prophet Isaiah prophesies in Isaiah chapter 53 what God incarnate will do.

> He was despised and rejected by mankind,
> a man of suffering, and familiar with pain.
> Like one from whom people hide their faces
> He was despised, and we held Him in low esteem.
> (Isaiah 53:3 NIV, emphasis mine)

Isaiah details one known as the Suffering Servant. Jesus did not arrive in pomp and circumstance. There was no royal procession. No heavenly army marched with Him into the city of Jerusalem. Jesus came as a fragile infant, fully dependent on the care of human parents. He is deeply familiar with the human experience. He understands pain; He understands suffering. The book of Hebrews says that Jesus was tempted as we are yet without sin.

> For we do not have a high priest who is unable to empathize with our weaknesses, but we have one who has been tempted in every way, just as we are—yet He did not sin. (Hebrews 4:15 NIV)

A man of sorrows acquainted with deepest grief. Tempted at all points as we are. This is Jesus—not a God of sympathy but of empathy.

We find throughout the Gospels Jesus being moved with compassion when seeing the suffering of humanity (Matthew 9:36, 14:14, 15:32, 18:27, 20:34; Mark 1:41, 6:34, 8:2; Luke 7:13, 15:20). The Greek word used for "compassion" in the above references is *splagchnizomai*, which means: "to be moved as to one's inwards."[4]

Jesus has such fierce compassion for broken humanity, that it moves Him to the core of His physical body. You're left with the mental image of Jesus doubled over in pain due to the suffering of humanity. This is Jesus—deeply acquainted with and hurt by what humanity suffers.

Weeping Jesus

One of my favorite stories in Scripture is recorded in the book of John, chapter 11. Prior to the story recorded here, Jesus has been healing all who are sick. Miraculous signs and wonders follow His ministry. Everywhere He goes, He overcomes impossible situations.

Jesus, the miracle worker.

Everywhere the Messiah travels teem with throngs of people. He has multitudes, He has followers, He has disciples, and He has friends.

Three of His friends are siblings named Mary, Martha, and Lazarus. One day, after Jesus has concluded teaching, He receives word from Mary and Martha that their brother—Jesus's dear friend Lazarus—is ill. Luckily, Lazarus is only a few miles away from where Jesus is. In a triumphal declaration, Jesus declares, "It happened for the glory of God so that the Son of God will receive glory from this" (John 11:4 NLT). I imagine His disciples fired up, high-fiving each other, chest bumping, accompanied with grunts of victory, while discussing the magnitude of the glory of God. Jesus speaks of glory as the reward—the goal—so, patience is required. Lazarus may be sick, but it is only a precursor to seeing God receive glory.

Yet, He waits two days.

And during the wait, Lazarus dies.

Is there glory in death?

When Jesus finally arrives in Bethany, Lazarus has already been in the tomb for four days. Mary and Martha are distraught. Their brother is dead, and the one who could have prevented it did not practice expedience. Martha meets Jesus on the road to air her grief. Mary can't even make her way out to see Jesus until He calls her out by name. They are dealing with pain, with grief, with loss. Their brother is dead.

Death is a permanent fixture.

Their hopes are dashed. Their faith seems misplaced.

Their belief that Jesus loved them must have seemed a mere illusion. How can a loving Messiah allow this? Allow death, allow pain, allow suffering? For His glory? How does that work?

Scripture records this exchange, and we are left with the gnawing feeling that Mary and Martha do not possess faith to believe in a physical resurrection for Lazarus.

We know the end of the story—keep in mind that they do not. To them, their brother is never coming back, and the only one who could have prevented this tragedy took a snow day.

Jesus could have rebuked them for their wavering faith. He could have scolded them for being closed minded and viewing things from a merely human perspective. But He doesn't do that. He reminds them who He is, and then something beautiful transpires. In the midst of a narrative ripe with agony and human suffering, we get one of the most emotive verses in Scripture:

> Jesus wept. (John 11:35 NIV)

His friend died. His other friends are heartbroken. Grief is all around Him; pain is in the air. A palpable feeling of loss and hopelessness grips the hearts of every bystander. The Savior, the Messiah, God incarnate, weeps.

Even knowing resurrection and glory are coming, Jesus slows His pace and allows pain to infiltrate His heart. He feels the very real emotions of grief, of compassion, of empathy. He knows resurrection will arrive, but that does not deter Him from feeling in the present. Mary, Martha, and the mourners weep, so Jesus weeps. He feels what we feel and responds accordingly.

When those around us weep, we are to weep. When those around us rejoice, we should rejoice. We are fashioned in the image and likeness of God. A God who weeps begets a Church that weeps. As followers of Christ, we are fashioned to live lives of empathy. Sympathy is cheap. Empathy is costly. We are to do our best to understand what we may never experience. If you are one who has never experienced an invisible illness, praise God—but do not settle for criticism and sympathy. You are called to empathize. Paul says it this way:

> Bear one another's burdens, and so fulfill the law of Christ. (Galatians 6:2 ESV)

The Greek is this: "bear" is *bastazo*, "to carry", "to bear", "to take away." "Burdens" is *baros*, "weight", or "burden", literally or metaphorically.

Paul is saying carry or take away the weight bearing down on your brothers and sisters in Christ. Invisible illnesses are weights. We are designed to do all we can to help carry that load. Bear with each other; share the weight. The book of Hebrews tells us to spur one another on in good works (Hebrews 10:24). *Spur* in Greek means "a provocation", which literally jabs, or cuts, someone so they *must* respond. It's a forceful pushing when we recognize someone slipping and remind them—urge them, implore them—to apprehend the call of God on their lives.

This is the call of the Church.

A call to empathy. To encouragement. To bear with one another and so fulfill the law of Christ.

Just because we know healing and resurrection are coming, it should not deter us from feeling today. We are to be present. Feel in the moment. Bear each other's burdens.

Let us be that Church.

CHAPTER 3

NATURE VS. NURTURE

> *What we achieve inwardly will change outer reality.*
>
> *—Author Uncertain*

My wife loves pickles to an unhealthy degree. I hate them. Despise them. I frown on the existence of whoever pickled the first cucumber. Because of your sin, sir or madam, local fast-food establishments have repeatedly soiled my order by not listening to my "hold-the-pickles" request.

One night, as every good husband does, I took my wife on what I thought was a romantic date. We took a stroll through midtown Sacramento and picked up some amazing third-wave coffee—by the way, Sacramento is famous for its exquisite coffee.[1] We are a blessed people in Northern California. My wife got her iced vanilla latte—correction: sweet latte, third-wave coffee shops don't "do" vanilla lattes. Ask for one and the barista will be sure to either educate you on your lack of coffee expertise or treat you to a look of disdain and disgust.

Depending on my mood, I will either grab a latte or an iced Americano. That night was an Americano night. After grabbing coffee, we walked hand in hand perusing local establishments, enjoying the chill provided by the autumn breeze coming off the American River. Sacramento is a great mixture of laid back and hustle. You get the artsy vibe of a big city without all the traffic and anxiety a city can incite. Sacramento boasts equal parts hipster, young business professional, and established family. One of our favorite spots is a burger joint known for their craft-brewed beer and juicy, heart-attack-inducing burgers. I'm a sucker for a good burger. We ordered, and we took our time talking, dating, and remembering why we fell in love in the first place.

Every time I order a burger, I am coerced into ordering "extra pickles" on the side, for you-know-who. On this occasion, the restaurant went above and beyond and gave us a mountain of pickles. My wife pounced on these distorted cucumbers. Her eyes widened, her mouth watering, the look of joy leaping off her face as she loudly, bluntly blurted out:

"These are the best pickles I have ever had!"

For the next hour, she proceeded to pester me until we went back to the chef to find out where they got their pickles and how we could obtain this delicacy. After some interrogation of the poor cooks, chefs, servers, busboys, Uber Eats drivers, and anyone my wife deemed "a regular", she got her info. On the way home, I happened to look over and see my wife on here phone, on the verge of spending fifty dollars on a jar of pickles. Fifty dollars on ONE JAR OF PICKLES.

One. Jar. Of. Pickles.

I did not allow that purchase to continue. *This addiction needs to end, I can't condone this sort of issue. I'm not an enabler.*

Pickles are gross. No one should like them. Yet the one I love has a problem—an addiction to them—and she has passed on her vice to my poor son. My question: Is this obsession a reflection of her genetic makeup or the result of some sort of horrible environmental factor?

As ridiculous as this illustration is, the question is real. Taste, likes, dislikes, preferences, pet peeves—are these the result of genetics or environmental factors? Many aspects of our humanity stem from nature, nurture, or a blend of both.

Nature vs. nurture can build an equation for diagnosing and analyzing many aspects of human behavior. But for our purposes, let's look at the causes of mental illnesses. The debate between determining human behavior on the basis of genetic predisposition or environmental influences goes back to 400 BCE.

Ancient History

Hippocrates, a Greek physician, was convinced from his observations that all human behavior was caused by biology—more specifically by four bodily fluids called humors.[2] The four humors he identified are:

- Yellow bile
- Blood
- Black bile
- Phlegm

Hippocrates and his followers believed that when the four humors were balanced within the body, health would follow. If the humors were misaligned or out of balance, in came disease and mental instability. The goal of these ancient Greeks was to align their lifestyles around maintaining the balance of the humors. Much of Greek medicine revolved around the humors, and medical diagnoses were simplified to reflect this source of balance. If a patient showed symptoms of depressive tendencies, physicians would assume black bile was in excess. Some physicians built upon these beliefs for centuries, while others believed factors outside of biology played a role in sickness and mental conditions.

One school of thought sprang into existence after Galen of Rome hinted at emotions and other factors as contributing to physical conditions. In one case, it is said that a woman showed up sick, but upon examination, no humor or physical conditions appeared to be the culprit. After careful examination, Galen determined the cause was emotional—she had a secret love interest. Galen believed in balancing the humors but introduced what he called the "non-naturals", some of which included "passions or perturbations of the soul". Moses Maimonides, a twelfth-century rabbi, philosopher, and physician, stated:

> It is known . . . that passions of the psyche produce changes in the body that are great, evident, and manifest to all. On this account . . . the movements of the psyche . . . should be kept in balance . . . and no other regimen should be given precedence.[3]

Galen helped to develop the doctrine of the non-naturals, which basically states physicians need to help patients deal with their emotions due to their physiological and mental effects. From this point in history on, medicine believed physical health was due to both emotional and natural issues—in laymen's terms, nature and nurture.

Throughout history, there has been debate on whether nature or nurture holds the most weight. Is sickness the result of biological conditions or the result of outside environmental influences? This debate lends itself to the field of mental health. As we dive into causality, I am by no means trying to suggest we are slaves to genetics or to our environment. We are not victims—we are victors. We overcome. We advance. However, oftentimes, to walk into victory we need to take a step back and determine how we got where we are.

TO WALK INTO VICTORY,
WE NEED TO TAKE A
STEP BACK AND
DETERMINE HOW WE
GOT TO WHERE WE ARE.

Sometimes the only way out is back through the muck and the mire of the past. In order to understand how we tick, we need to know why we tick the way we tick. Are mental illnesses caused by biology or by life experiences? Is it one or the other, or is it both? Let's take a look.

Nature

One of my favorite movies of all time is the original *Jurassic Park*. Very few films seamlessly weave wonder, imagination, horror, violence, love, and kid-like excitement into a mosaic of awesomeness. In the movie, a character named Dennis Nedry, is a greedy IT genius who accidently turns loose a bunch of prehistoric, man-eating reptiles. In one scene, we see Dennis in a control room, computers and technology everywhere. He locks down certain protocols to buy some time to make a buck. Things go horribly wrong, and Mr. Nedry gets a faceful of poison spit before becoming a dino-nugget.

The control center controls the entirety of Jurassic Park. One rogue employee in the control center produces devastating results.

Our brains are the control centers of our bodies; if our brains are off, the rest of us is off. If our brains aren't in a healthy space, it will have devastating results on the entirety of our lives and the lives of those around us. An "off" brain can produce invisible illness.

Thomas R. Insel, MD, director of the National Institute of Mental Health, is on the front lines of medical research that holds that mental illness is a product of biology and environment. He stresses the importance of viewing mental illness with the same lens through which we may view heart disease or diabetes.

> The only difference here is that the organ of interest is the brain instead of the heart or pancreas. But the same basic principles apply.[4]

Insel argues that cardiovascular health was in its infancy a century ago. Physicians did not have the necessary tools to diagnose the real issue. Similarly, today, we are in the infancy of understanding brain health, but there is hope on the horizon.

Biology and genetics play a role in mental disorders. Scientists have found genes that are linked to schizophrenia and PTSD. These genes, when exposed to the right circumstances, manifest themselves as invisible illness. Almost daily, new scientific studies are being conducted on the function and dysfunction of the brain. One study conducted by Helen Mayberg, MD,[5] professor of psychiatry and neurology at Emory University, identified an area of the human brain entitled Brodmann area 25. The study concluded that Brodmann area 25 was overactive in individuals experiencing depression. With the proper amount of "deep-brain stimulation", some relief was found.

If our brains are the control center of our bodies, one wrong entry could cause mass chaos to the rest of the network. Some invisible illnesses are connected to an imbalance of chemicals in the brain called neurotransmitters. Neurotransmitters are the nerve connectors in the brain. If the nerves do not connect, vital messages don't flow as they should. If vital messages don't flow as they should, invisible illnesses could ensue. If you have an imbalance of neurotransmitters, various expressions of mental illness could result.

Most psychologists and doctors agree on a few basic groups of genetic predispositions, or things that have the power to alter the chemistry, resulting in invisible illness. We will discuss those here, but please note that this is not an all-inclusive list.

Heredity

In 2019, my wife and I had our first baby. I'll never forget looking at his chubby little ET-ish face for the first time. Every father knows the inexpressible love you feel the first time you snuggle your baby. I recall counting his fingers and his toes, and carefully examining his ears, just to make sure everything was all there. Quickly, I began to notice features that resembled me and features that resembled my wife.

"He has your eyes!"

"He has your feet."

"His finger is crooked like yours!"

Genetics is amazing. Genes are passed on from one generation to the next. Much of who we are is passed through our family lines. Just like our physical attributes are passed from parents to offspring, invisible illnesses can be passed on.

In my family of origin, most of us have dealt with varying levels of depression. My wife and her siblings often have conversations regarding their experiences with mental illness.

The National Institutes of Health states it this way: "Scientists have long recognized that many psychiatric disorders tend to run in families.... Such disorders include autism, attention deficit hyperactivity disorder (ADHD), bipolar disorder, major depression, and schizophrenia."[6] Researchers and doctors alike are seeing commonality in mental illnesses within families. It's probable that if you suffer from an invisible illness, someone else in your family of origin does as well. Studies are showing multiple generations afflicted with the same mental illnesses, but they may vary in the severity or the manifestation of their symptoms.[7] There is even evidence to suggest certain ailments skip generations and pop up later on.

Another study compiled research from multiple outlets and drew up the probabilities of dealing with schizophrenia or bipolar disorder. An average person has a one-out-of-one-hundred chance of developing schizophrenia or bipolar disorder. If one parent has schizophrenia, the chances become six out of one hundred. If one of the parents has bipolar disorder, the chances escalate to ten out of one hundred. If both biological parents have schizophrenia, the chances skyrocket to forty-five out of one hundred and forty out of one hundred for bipolar disorder.[8]

Just like we inherit wonderful features, such as eye color, stature, and sense of humor, we can inherit traits that are not as positive, such as heart issues, slow metabolism, and, yes, even mental illness.

Mariel Hemmingway details in a Q & A for *Counseling Today* her experience with invisible illness, recounting a family lineage that includes seven suicides—including that of her grandfather, Ernest Hemingway—along with depression, addiction, and various eating disorders. When asked what she was planning to share in an upcoming speech, she summarizes: "I'll talk about how creative and blessed they were and also how haunted they were by life, addiction, fears, etc. I relate it to my own fears, triumphs, and failures, and how I have used mindfulness and lifestyle (food, nature, exercise, water, sleep, and laughter) as a way to find balance and joy in my life."[9] Obviously, her family life is at the extreme end of the spectrum, but it serves to show that invisible illnesses can, in fact, be hereditary. As we move towards healing, we must take inventory of the possible pitfalls that lurk in our genetics.

Infections

Infections can alter "what could have been". Various studies have concluded that childhood infections can result in childhood and adult mental illness.[10] Infections can cause brain damage, and brain damage can in turn lead to a decrease of functionality in the brain. One known condition in children called "pediatric autoimmune neuropsychiatric disorder (PANDA) associated with Streptococcus (Strep) bacteria has been linked to obsessive-compulsive disorder (OCD) and other mental illnesses in children."[11]

An extensive study in Denmark found a significant link between infections and invisible illnesses like schizophrenia, depression, and bipolar disorder.[12]

After researchers looked into the hospitalization and prescription data on "more than 1 million children born in Denmark between 1995 and 2012 using two national registries", researchers concluded that there was a correlation between infections and mental illness.

> The data revealed that infections requiring hospitalizations were associated with an 84% increased risk of a mental health disorder diagnosis in the hospital setting and a 42% increased risk in the use of psychotropic medications.[13]

Norbert Müller of the Department of Psychiatry and Psychotherapy of the University of Munich concluded in a lengthy study that he would "support the view that infection, psychoneuroimmunology, and inflammation rightly should be a focus of psychiatric research", due to their correlation to mental illness.[14]

Science is showing a link between infections that affect one's brain and the likelihood of that individual experiencing mental illness as an adult.

Injuries to the Brain

My parents are from Arkansas. I was born and raised in the Sacramento area of California, and it's safe to say the culture on the West Coast is a tad bit different from the southeastern part of the United States. The people who taught me how to talk speak with a Southern twang. So I, in turn, was a kid from Sacramento with a Southern twang. Was I from the South? Nope. But my linguistic styling was passed down from my parents.

My dad also passed down an absolute obsession with football. In the South, football is a religion. Millions of dollars are sacrificed at the altar of football every year, be it NFL or NCAA football. One of my favorite times of year is late August to early September. Why? The start of football season—and I LOVE watching football with my dad.

However, a few years back, a movie based on a true story came out entitled *Concussion*. This movie has tainted how I view and enjoy football to this day. Will Smith plays Dr. Bennet Omalu, the doctor who discovered the link between football, concussions sustained during football, and the disease Chronic Traumatic Encephalopathy (CTE). Dr. Bennet Omalu began to investigate the brains of deceased NFL players after reports of erratic behavior and suicidal ideation.

Today, we know the long-term effects of multiple concussions can lead to CTE. Some of the effects of CTE are

> memory loss, confusion, impaired judgment, impulse-control problems, aggression, depression, anxiety, suicidality, parkinsonism, and, eventually, progressive dementia. These symptoms often begin

years or even decades after the last brain trauma or end of active athletic involvement.[15]

The discovery of CTE is just one example of how brain trauma can be the catalyst for mental illness. Sustaining head trauma can disrupt the synthesis and balance of chemicals, as well as interfering with normal brain function.

One Danish study has shown that sustaining head injuries can bolster the potential for developing certain mental illnesses by 439 percent.[16] In this study, scientists studied 1.4 million Danes born between 1977 and 2000 and continued investigating these individuals until 2010. Out of the 113,906 individuals who were hospitalized from head trauma, this study found that those with head injuries were:

> 65 percent more likely to be diagnosed with schizophrenia
>
> 59 percent more likely to develop depression
>
> 28 percent more likely to be diagnosed with bipolar disorder
>
> 439 percent more likely to suffer from organic mental disorders[17]

Stateside, the NIH found that "approximately one in five individuals may experience mental health symptoms up to six months after mild traumatic brain injury."[18] Events, injuries, and trauma can affect the chemistry of the brain and result in mental illness.

So, we see that nature—both heredity and factors that can affect the biology and chemistry of the brain—can predispose individuals to mental illness.

Nurture

Nurture refers to all the environmental variables that impact who we are, including our early childhood experiences, how we were raised, our social relationships, and our surrounding culture.[19]

Every individual has a different path that has led to their current reality. Their current position in life is the sum of their decisions, circumstances, environments, culture, and genetics. Take out genetics from that list, and we are left with the complex variables associated with nurture. Varying levels of invisible illness can be spurred on by environmental factors encompassed in the word *nurture*. Again, the nature vs. nurture debate is ultimately asking the question: Is biology to blame for invisible illness, or is it the sum of decisions, experiences, and environments someone is exposed to?

Those who assist others in coping with mental illness agree that the following factors can play a role in the manifestation of invisible illness.

Abuse

Studies have shown that physical, mental, and sexual abuse can play roles in the development of mental illness. Adults who have lived through abuse face what may feel like an uphill battle in apprehending a shred of normalcy. In the United States, close to twenty people are abused per minute. The math adds up to nearly ten million individuals per year walking through abuse.[20] Needless to say, quite a few of us are carrying baggage. We have seen things we never should have seen, and things have been done to us that never should have been done. When we suffer abuse, especially from someone close— someone trusted—our mental well-being is affected. When trust is broken, our minds suffer.

Consensus within the medical community shows: "Persisting mental health problems are a common consequence of child abuse and neglect in adults."[21] Unfortunately, abuse is common in our world, and its effects on our minds may be greater than we realize.

For a moment, let's specifically focus on sexual abuse.

Heretohelp is an organization designed to provide aid in mental health and substance abuse. They found:

> Childhood sexual abuse can have a wide range of effects in adulthood. Some adult survivors experience few mental health problems, while others experience many mental health problems. Abuse is a kind of trauma. Trauma is a situation that's shocking, intense, and distressing.[22]

They discuss some of the possible long-term effects on the well-being of adults living with sexual abuse, such as issues related to trust and self-esteem, stress, impulsivity, anger, dissociation, and self-harm. Studies are clear—sexual abuse has massive ramifications on a person's mental well-being.[23]

Sexual abuse isn't like other forms of abuse. Scripture is clear on the underbelly of sexual misconduct. Sexual misconduct has the potential to affect the whole of an individual more than any other human conduct. God designed sex to be beautiful. Within the proper context, sex is a binding agent between a husband and wife. Jesus refers to this in the Gospel of Mark:

> But at the beginning of creation God "made them male and female". "For this reason a man will leave his father and mother and be *united* to his wife, and the two will become *one flesh*." So they are no longer two, *but one flesh*. Therefore what God has joined together, let no one separate. (Mark 10:6–9 NIV, emphasis mine)

When Jesus refers to the two becoming one, He is speaking physiologically, spiritually, and emotionally. Sexual acts have the power to render permanent results. This reality can be beautiful within the context of Biblical marriage. Outside that context, sex can be damaging.

Sex is like a fire. Fire can be used for warmth, comfort, and to provide the power to cultivate necessities. Very few things are more relaxing than sitting around a fire with family and close friends, discussing life and the goodness of God. Fire is designed to be beautiful and useful. Similarly, sex is designed to bring a husband and wife to oneness as a type and picture of Jesus and His Bride, the Church.

Sex is a great thing.

However, like fire, that very same flame used for warmth, comfort, and to provide the power to cultivate necessities can be utilized to instigate total and complete destruction. Outside of the confines of a fireplace, the same fire can burn the whole house down. A great thing in the wrong context is destructive.

We see horrific evidence of this in the lives of so many victims. Sexual misconduct is traumatic and can often lead victims into a battle with invisible illness. Overall, those who have endured abuse have a greater likelihood of experiencing mental illness.

Stress

Stress is defined as:

1. Pressure or tension exerted on a material object

2. A state of mental or emotional strain or tension resulting from adverse or very demanding circumstances

Unbridled stress can also contribute to various mental illnesses. According to the dictionary definition, stress is a state of mental or emotional strain, tension, or pressure. If you've lived any amount of life on planet earth, you know that stress is a part of it. However, certain life events cause a destructive amount of stress in our lives. Loss, family life, and finances can be the biggest causes of stress. Let's look at each of these.

Loss. When I was in high school, one of my good friends was a giant of a man. He was one of those fifteen-year-old kids with a full beard—six foot two and the deepest voice you've ever heard. He was the guy no one wanted to line up against on the football field—he might just figuratively or literally kill you. One day, I saw him walking with his shoulder crooked, doing his best inadvertent Quasimodo impersonation. He briefly explained that he was fine but felt a "little" pinch. This legend sought no medical help and played out the remainder of the season, only to find out he had been playing with a broken collarbone and torn rotator cuff the ENTIRE season. A giant of a man ... boy ... man-boy.

We played football together, graduated together, and spent a good amount of time causing mischief and running from the consequences together. As often happens, we went different ways after graduation. I went on to an intern program in a different city, and he stayed local. We fell out of touch for the most part, with brief interactions through social media every now and then. I started to hear whispers that my friend was dealing with severe depression. This giant of a man was being made small by malfunctions in his brain.

One morning, while browsing Facebook, my heart sank into my chest. I paused, read, reread, and reread again. My friend, the man-boy, had taken his own life at twenty-one years old. He had all the potential in the world, all the gifting you could ever desire, but his mind wasn't right. I'll never forget that moment, it was one of the first times in my adult life that I experienced real loss. Real, heartbreaking, speechless loss. Loss is devastating. Loss is stressful.

The National Center for Biotechnology Information found a correlation between loss and invisible illness:

> Unexpected death was the most common traumatic experience and most likely to be rated as the respondent's worst, regardless of other traumatic experiences. Increased incidence after unexpected death was observed at every point across the life course for major depressive episodes, panic disorder, and post-traumatic stress disorder.[24]

Loss brings about stress, and stress can incite mental illness. Loss, grief, and their effects are brutal to cope with, to say the least.

Family Life. Our families of origin can also cause undue stress that can manifest in mental illness. Families are messy. The reality is not all of us start out of the blocks in life. Some get a head start, and some have a handicap. The way you were raised, your nuclear family—or lack thereof—can have adverse effects on mental health. God designed families to be the basic building blocks for society. We were created to be in tight-knit relationships with those we call family. When those relationships are strained, stress can occur and produce various mental illnesses. Secular research is showing how vital strong family units are to vibrant mental health.[25]

An increasing body of research demonstrates that negative family relationships can cause stress, impact mental health, and even cause physical symptoms. Non-supportive families can detract from mental health and/or cause a mental illness to worsen.

Dr. Anne-Marie Conn from the University of Rochester Medical Center has researched ties between mental health in children and the stability or instability of their home lives and found that dysfunctional upbringings are very much tied to psychological damage.[26]

The way we are raised has repercussions on our mental health. Maybe the reason you are unable to cope with stress as an adult is due to the stress you were consistently under as a child. Maybe your inability to cope with the feeling of "being enough" is due to not having your value validated by loving parents. Homelife and continued family life into adulthood have an array of effects on our mental health.

Finances. I'm sure no one reading this has ever encountered stress related to finances. I don't know about you, but I wake up every day and pull a Scrooge McDuck as I dive into my pool of Benjamins. I find myself pulling quarters out of my pockets hours after my dip in mountains of cash. It's a heavy burden, but it's mine to bear. Okay, that's obviously not true—I'm in ministry.

We have all dealt with stress in our finances in one way or another. In fact, the APA (American Psychological Association) records that 72 percent of adults indicate they carry stress regarding their financial well-being.[27]

The pursuit of financial health is stressful and consuming. When finances are unhealthy, it becomes increasingly difficult to maintain health in other areas of life. Solomon got it right in Proverbs, stating, "The borrower is slave to the lender." Very few things steal freedom like debt and an inability to create wealth. Financial hardship can create a prison of despair, depression, and anxiety that feels inescapable.

I've been laid off twice due to corporate acquisitions. During corporate takeovers, the immediate collateral damage is usually in the personnel department. The first time this occurred, I had been married less than a year, and we were making peanuts already. Very few things are as emasculating as telling your new wife you are unable to provide and pay rent. In my case, depression followed each layoff.

I'm not the only one. Finances can cause stress, and unchecked stress is invariably linked to mental illness.

Trauma

All of these factors flow together to compose nurture and can largely be boiled down to trauma. Trauma is simply a distressing or disturbing experience. Anything that causes distress and disturbance can be classified as trauma. Which means we are all running around with varying levels of trauma. Some of us have been carrying years and years of horrific trauma and don't even recognize it. It may be too painful to even revisit. Trauma can often be like the junk drawer—you know it needs to be dealt with, but it's overwhelming. Often, we don't realize the power trauma can have over our minds and our bodies. We weren't designed to function with unresolved issues.

Sometimes, our brains black out moments of trauma. For years, I subconsciously buried the sexual assault I experienced as a child. One day, while at an intensive healing event, it was as if God reminded me of the trauma I experienced. When I began to dive into that trauma, I began to find some healing. Let's not ignore the pain in an effort to remain comfortable. Healing comes when we embrace the past and seek to move forward.

As we can see, our nurture plays a large role in determining our level of mental stability.

Not One or the Other—Both

So, which one is it? Is nature or is nurture responsible for our invisible illness? The answer isn't as clear-cut as most of us would like; all of the research resounds with both and—that is, both our nature and our nurture play a part in our mental health and the manifestation of our invisible illness.

Think of your biology as an envelope and mental illness as the letter inside the envelope. The nurture side of the equation is the action of opening the envelope. Just because someone has a genetic predisposition towards invisible illness does not mean they will experience it. The genetic predisposition is a letter that can be left unread if not exposed to the "opening" environmental factors. Some of us have genetic predispositions that may never manifest themselves, and some of us have those same genetic predispositions and, when exposed to the right environmental conditions, voilà! Invisible illness occurs. The genetic predisposition individuals may have towards mental illness can be activated by various environmental factors.

Due to my family line and the vast array of those related to me who have dealt with invisible illness, I believe I was genetically predisposed to mental illness. The sexual abuse I encountered, mixed with a variety of other stimuli, opened the letter. The mental illness I experience today is the result of both my nature and my nurture—that is, both genetic predisposition and exposure to environmental factors.

Now that we have this info, what do we do about it? Many of us haven't exactly won the genetic lottery, and life has thrown its fair share of curveballs. What do we do with the hands we have been dealt? Well, that is the point of this book. Keep reading. We will talk about some practicalities in the next few chapters. But, as stated earlier, in order to move forward, we needed to understand how we got where we are.

Putting a Bow on It

I used to be in the solar business. My job was to manage the project managers. I would regularly connect salespeople to the document-generation team to the utility team to the install crew. My job was to be the "unsticker." Installing solar panels is a construction project, and the vast majority of construction projects have a slew of red tape and permits to go through. I was tasked with pushing everything through as quickly as possible from the point of sale to the solar panels powering the home. I was good at it, so I got promoted to managing and training teams. Consistently, I would see agents deal with the headaches of the job but not take enough time to ensure the cause of the issue was addressed. We began to teach and train our agents to use a method called root-cause analysis. The goal of this method is simple: don't treat the symptoms, treat the actual root issue. If you correct the root issue, the symptoms oftentimes go the way of the buffalo. Our agents would find an issue in each job and ask the question; Why? Typically, "Why?" was asked seven times before the real why was revealed. We saw a massive improvement in every measurable metric. Our people were trained not to numb the pain but to continue to push until they found the why behind the what.

The purpose of this entire chapter is not to attack any sense of hope you may have; the goal is to open a window into your soul. We need to understand why we deal with what we deal with or why our loved ones deal with what they deal with. Invisible illnesses are symptoms of larger hidden issues. For true transformation, we need to do a root-cause analysis—we need to deal with the root of the issues. We need to push past the desperate tendency to want to simply numb the pain. Instead, we need to strive for complete wholeness. God has designed us to be whole. Wholeness is a process; let's not rush through the process. Understanding the *why* behind the *what* often reveals the best course of action to achieve the wholeness we desire.

Our nature—our biological makeup, and our nurture—our life experiences, each play a role in our mental health. Take a minute to do a root-cause analysis on yourself. Be honest, be real, and be raw. Here are some questions to ask:

- How was my childhood *really*?
- How are my stress levels? Are family, finances, or loss causing too much stress?
- Is there any abuse from my past that I haven't dealt with?
- Are there any medical conditions that could be playing a role in my mental health?
- Are there generational issues that could be affecting my mental health?
- Am I working through these real issues in order to thrive?

Asking these questions and answering them honestly can help to cultivate an action plan for solid mental health. Biology is only one factor; environment is only one factor. It is vital to purposely reject ignorance and embrace action. Let's do the hard work that needs to be done in order to thrive with anxiety and depression.

PART TWO: TRIGGERS

PART 2

TRIGGERS

> *Do not conform to the pattern of this world but be transformed by the renewing of your mind. Then you will be able to test and approve what God's will is—his good, pleasing and perfect will.*
>
> *Romans 12:2*

Growing up in a large family has benefits and drawbacks. Now, don't get me wrong—I love my siblings. We are super close to this day, but no one knows how to push you to the brink of murder like siblings. Some might say we are stubborn. I prefer to think we ooze leadership potential. Strong opinions, snide remarks, backhanded compliments, and sarcastic quips are beautifully pieced together to form a dialogue between the four Taylor siblings. Linguistic gymnastics are essential to cut into our conversations. I've heard it said healthy conversations resemble an organized game of volleyball; with each person getting their turn, while setting up the others. Our conversations look more like racquetball—the ball wildly flying around, as the players forcefully drive it off every corner. You had better take caution—you never know when the ball is coming for your head. It's all in good fun, we love it, and we wouldn't have it any other way.

My parents really liked each other, and kept popping out babies close together after I was born. To reiterate (because it will annoy my younger siblings if they read this), I am the eldest of the four. I've had a total of about eighteen months out of my whole life when the responsibility of leadership was *not* squarely on my shoulders.

Most of the time growing up, we were all the best of friends. But there were moments when I would read the story of Joseph in Genesis, carefully dissecting how his brothers got away with selling him, and I would ponder whether I could recreate that scenario without losing Super Nintendo privileges. After much deliberation, I concluded that it was too risky; there was too much NBA Jam to be played.

Aaron is second in birth order. We grew up doing everything together. He has always been bigger and hairier than me, and was frequently mistaken for the eldest. Throughout our lives, we engaged in what we called our "biannual fights". Most of the time, we were all about baseball, basketball, and razor scooters galore, but that guy knows how to say just the right things to ignite the beast in me. We would go from building bunk beds to WWE Smackdown in ten seconds flat.

"*How?*" you might ask. Usually, it was one word or one phrase that would set one of us off. In laymen's terms, it was a trigger. The definition of a *trigger* is as follows:

1. *noun*: a small device that releases a spring or catch, and so sets off a mechanism, especially in order to fire a gun.

2. *verb*: to cause (an event or situation) to happen or exist

Triggers release things.

Triggers cause things.

Triggers set things in motion.

All of us have triggers for various things. We have things that trigger anger, sex drive, sadness, and happiness. There are also triggers for invisible illnesses. It is vital to understand what triggers an episode. Understanding triggers is vital to maintaining a life of stability of mind.

The previous three chapters dealt a lot with history, personal examples, and anecdotes. Now we move on to triggers, and the practical struggle for a life of mental stability. By no means will we be able to cover every trigger—this is not an exhaustive list. We will cover some basic triggers and some coping mechanisms I use in my life and ones I have seen used by people much wiser than I. The goal is simply to inspire you to find *your* triggers, or for you, who care for someone with invisible illness, to identify their triggers in order to better manage their symptoms. At the end of the day, God has entrusted life, purpose, and an opportunity to make an eternal difference to each of us. What we do with what we have been given is vital in order to step into the fullness of life made available by the finished work of the cross.

One thing I want to emphasize with triggers is that mitigating them may not completely eradicate the effects of mental illness. Even by stewarding physical, relational, and spiritual triggers, we may still experience the ramifications of our invisible illness. However, managing triggers is still beneficial in the long run. We do our best to manage what we have been given and trust that God, doctors, our medication, and a good therapist can help with the rest.

In the life of every believer, we are to balance wisdom with faith. Faith believes for a greater tomorrow, while wisdom takes practical steps to be a good steward today. Faith claims healing and peace of mind, while wisdom deals with triggers as you navigate the wait for healing. Faith declares God's goodness and sufficiency, while wisdom cultivates the brain God entrusted to you. Faith and wisdom, wisdom and faith—two sides to the same coin.

Too often, people move in presumption and not faith. They presume there is healing for their minds in the immediate, so they do not take care of themselves. They eat foods that are poison to the mind, they fill their spirits with garbage entertainment, and they engage in toxic relationships. Then they end up disillusioned and mad at God for not coming through. God is sovereign and, in His sovereignty, He will allow you to reap the fruit of your decisions. If you do not manage triggers well, you will reap a harvest of mental instability.

"Everything happens for a reason" is an oft-quoted saying that many believe is in Scripture and use as a license to live like fools. I'm not saying I entirely disagree with the sentiment. But perhaps the reason you are where you are is a lack of wisdom, resulting in really dumb decisions compounded over time. We are to live by faith yet exercise wisdom in the process.

Wisdom and faith, faith and wisdom.

Wisdom learns about and navigates triggers. What triggers your mental illness and what triggers mine may be vastly different, but we must know our triggers to conquer or circumnavigate them. For me, hunger, loneliness, poor eating, lack of exercise, and failure are triggers to depression. Unresolved conflict, unmet expectations, and fear of rejection all trigger my anxiety. It has taken years and difficult introspection to understand my triggers, but that effort has made all the difference.

In this section, we will cover physical, spiritual, and emotional triggers. We will paint with a broad brush in order to cover a variety of triggers. My prayer is that we may see triggers for what they are: an opportunity for growth. Let's grow together and in so doing bring glory to God.

CHAPTER 4

PHYSICAL TRIGGERS

> *If you don't take care of your body, where are you going to live?*
>
> —*Unknown*

I had dreams of being over six feet tall. I grew up watching and obsessing over "His Airness", Michael Jordan. The '90s was a time of bright colors, bad pants, patchy mustaches, and, of course, Michael Jordan. Space Jam was *my* jam. "I Believe I Can Fly" often provided the soundtrack for an evening spent with a lowered basketball hoop and attempts to dunk from the free-throw line like my idol. I would be the white Mike—*just make it to six feet.*

My dad is six foot three, and I have uncles that are giants. I thought my chances were pretty good that height was in the cards. Unfortunately, I got my five-foot-two mother's genes. I stand at a towering five foot ten ... and a half.

Don't leave out the *"and a half."*

That matters.

My two little brothers are about six foot. My little sister is five foot nine-ish. I'm the eldest and the runt. Surprisingly, my towering physique was rescued by a growth spurt in high school. As a freshman, my existence was that of a five-foot-two, 120-pound teenager.

I'm not exactly a physical specimen, yet I try my best to take care of the body I have. That has not always been true. At one point, I subscribed to the bachelor diet of 80 percent dirty carbs and 20 percent sugar and wondered why I felt like the inside of a toilet bowl. I have since educated myself and changed my lifestyle.

What is often perplexing to me is how people are unable to see how vital it is to take care of the body they have been given. We have one life and one body, and we had better take its upkeep seriously. Often, those who struggle with invisible illness neglect their physical health. If physical health is not a priority, those who suffer from various mental illnesses can be triggered more often than they would like. What you do with your body matters for your mental well-being.

All aspects of our lives are interconnected. We are made up of body, soul, and spirit. Your body affects your soul, which in turn affects your spirit, and vice versa. I'll say it again in a different way to make sure we are on the same page.

All that makes you *you* is interconnected. What you do with your body and what you use as fuel for your body will trigger what happens in your head.

Physical triggers are real, and we had better pay attention to our bodies.

The Bible on Physical Maintenance

Let's get physical, physical. How you maintain and take care of your body matters to God. Let's first consider that the way we look, how we are shaped and designed are the handiwork of God. David exclaims in Psalm 139:

> For you created my inmost being;
>
> you knit me together in my mother's womb.
>
> I praise you because I am fearfully and wonderfully made;
>
> your works are wonderful,
>
> I know that full well. (Psalm 139:13–14 NIV)

In verse 13, David uses the Hebrew word *qanah* for "formed." *Qanah* can be translated as "to erect", "to create." The word "knit" is *sakhakh*, which means "to screen", "to cover", "to join together."

PSALM 139:13-14 NIV

"FOR YOU CREATED
MY INNERMOST
BEING; YOU KNIT
ME TOGETHER IN
MY MOTHER'S
WOMB. I PRAISE
YOU BECAUSE I AM
FEARFULLY AND
WONDERFULLY
MADE; YOUR
WORKS ARE
WONDERFUL,
I KNOW THAT
FULL WELL."

In verse 14, before praising God for all of this, David states he is "fearfully and wonderfully made." *Fearfully* refers to causing astonishment and awe, and *wonderfully* refers to being separated or distinct. Let's put all this together:

God created your inmost being and joined you together in your mother's womb. What He made causes astonishment and awe and is distinct. This should lead you to a place of total worship as you reflect on the beauty of God's masterful workmanship.

What a beautiful concept.

You were formed by God, imagined by God, designed by God for God. The by-product should be praise and adoration for God from His creation.

Let's look at Genesis and creation. God speaks, and light bursts onto the scene. He then continues to design sunsets and sunrises constraining both day and night. Picture the moon and the sun placed by the very hands of God while He breathes the stars into existence. Then a divide is placed between the heavens and the waters of the earth. Days pass, and the creativity of God is made manifest in the great variety of wildlife that springs forth. As the words leave the lips of God, life cascades into existence.

Yet, something is missing. In the glory of creation and in the majesty of His art, an image bearer is not found. The whole of creation is created from the words of God—save one.

Humanity.

With humanity, we get a very different scene.

> Then God said, "Let Us make mankind in Our
> image, in Our likeness, so that they may rule over
> the fish in the sea and the birds in the sky, over the
> livestock and all the wild animals, and over all the
> creatures that move along the ground."
> So God created mankind in His own image,
> in the image of God He created them;
> male and female He created them. (Genesis 1:26–27
> NIV)

More detail is given on the intricacies of the creation of
mankind.

> Then the LORD God formed a man from the dust of
> the ground and breathed into his nostrils the breath
> of life, and the man became a living being. (Genesis
> 2:7 NIV)

With man, God does not *speak* existence. With man, God
formed, and God *breathed*. As a potter spends time forming
his clay into a masterpiece, so Yahweh spent time and intention
forming the body of humanity, and then breathed life. This is a
picture of intimacy, of care from the Creator for His creation.

Not only did humanity receive the time and care and very
breath of God in forming and bringing us to life, but we were
endowed with the image and likeness of God. We are image
bearers. The *imago Dei*. As image bearers, we are to reflect the

very glory of God. Just as statues remind us of the *real deal*, so we who bear God's image should remind the whole of creation of the beauty of God.

Let me illustrate what I mean.

I am a massive Sacramento Kings fan. It's an unfortunate, depraved life that I live, to be sure. I often tell people that being a Kings fan is what it must feel like to have an ugly child—you just hope puberty comes, and there is some development. Unfortunately, basketball puberty has lasted fourteen years for the Kings. I know, that's cold, but that is *my* truth. A part of loving the Sacramento Kings is loathing the Los Angeles Lakers. *Lakers* is a cuss word in my household. They disgust me and cause me to dry heave. I'm sure the players are great people, but their team was conceived from the loins of Satan. (Don't quote me on that—that is not a Biblical truth.)

The entrance to the home of the Lakers, the Staples Center, is littered with statues of Lakers legends such as Shaquille O'Neal, Kareem Abdul-Jabbar, Magic Johnson, and Jerry West. The purpose of those statues is not for visitors to simply admire the craftsmanship of the sculptures. The goal is to bring to remembrance the greatness of the individuals whose images the statues represent. Even if they are, well, Lakers.

As we live our lives, the goal is not to absorb glory but to reflect and bring to remembrance the greatness of the One whose image we bear. So that means, in every arena, what we do with what we have been given is a big deal.

How you develop your holiness matters.
How you steward your finances matters.
How you treat people matters.
How you love your spouse and children matters.
How you care for the body you have been given matters.
It all matters. It's bigger than you and me and our preferences;
it's about reflecting glory.

Your body was not an afterthought. Yet, so many Christians treat their bodies as disconnected entities. Again, the whole of our beings—soul, spirit, and body—is interconnected. If you do not treat your body well, there are ramifications on other facets of your being.

Paul wrote a letter to the church in Corinth, addressing a variety of things, one being sexual immorality and the importance of temple maintenance.

> Do you not know that your bodies are temples of the Holy Spirit, who is in you, whom you have received from God? You are not your own; you were bought at a price. Therefore honor God with your bodies. (1 Corinthians 6:19–20 NIV)

Paul is addressing individuals having casual sex with temple prostitutes and claiming, "No harm no foul." Corinth was a melting pot of ethnicities, cultures, and ideologies. The Corinthians took great pride in their knowledge and intellectual prowess. In watching the lives of many Corinthian Christians, Paul sees cognitive dissonance between their faith and their actions, which sounds the alarm for the apostle to speak into the true meaning of Christian liberty. Into this context, Paul pens, "Do you not know that your bodies are temples of the Holy Spirit?"

Paul is highlighting the price Jesus paid for salvation and Lordship and applying it to how we use our bodies. Paul insists, *"You are not your own; you were bought at a price. Therefore, honor God with your bodies."*

Honor God with your bodies.
In my sex life, honor God.
In my eating habits, honor God.
In my exercise, honor God.

What I am not doing is defining what *honor* means; what I am doing is attempting to shed some light on an often-overlooked side of our spirituality—taking care of our bodies. Being a good steward of your body is honoring to God. By refusing to take care of yourself physically, you dishonor the temple God gave you, and you are withholding honor due to God. God spent time creating, knitting, and forming us. We have been made temples of the Holy Spirit; we had best take care of ourselves.

When we stiff-arm good stewardship in the physical, we reap not only physical, but often mental repercussions.

Personal Application

I write this section of the book amid the Covid-19 pandemic of 2020. Before this pandemic, I had a home gym in my garage, and I did my best to utilize it four or five times per week. Since the pandemic, my wife and I sold our home, moved all of our stuff (including my gym equipment) into storage, and moved in with relatives.

There is a phenomenon that transpires with incoming college freshmen called the "Freshman 15." Basically, hordes of young people put on fifteen pounds during their freshman year. Let's just draw a parallel in a moment of transparency and say I have put on the "Quarantine 15." Without my gym equipment, and with all other fitness centers closed due to the virus, I have allowed myself to trade a barbell for a Marie Calendar Oreo Crust Coconut Cream Pie, and it shows. I've pushed my summer body to June 2021.

With a lack of physical discipline and giving little to no attention to my physical health (both exercise and nutrition), I've noticed my mental health has taken a turn for the worse. I'm not downplaying other factors, such as isolation, pastoring in a pandemic, and the attrition of parishioners, but as I have allowed my physical health to slip, my mental health has gone with it. I find myself battling depression more often than I have in the past few years. My anxiety, at times, is through the roof. I'm unable to cope with the normal stresses of marriage and family and have found myself being short with my wife more often than I would like to admit. Managing and stewarding our physical health to the best of our abilities oftentimes directly correlates to our mental health and ability to manage invisible illness.

For many of us, poor physical maintenance is a trigger for episodes of mental illness. We have to understand the biological consequences of not exercising and eating well. Keep in mind, your brain is the control center, and the food you eat is full of chemicals. Working out also releases chemicals, and not working out withholds those chemicals. If you input the wrong chemicals into the control center, or don't input the correct ones, things happen. What we do with our bodies—how we steward the physical—is directly connected to the processes in our mind. Neglect of the physical is a trigger, plain and simple.

Science Said It

The medical community has quite a bit to say about the importance of nutrition and working out. If you watch any amount of television, you will see numerous advertisements urging you to remember the importance of living an active lifestyle. Over the last several decades, active lifestyles and entertainment requiring physical exertion have been replaced by binge-watching Netflix, catching *Lost* on Hulu, and playing the latest and greatest version of *Halo*. We have traded physical fitness for convenience.

Another contributing factor is the evolution of work. As Western societies have migrated further and further from a primary blue-collar workforce to more sedentary jobs, our health has suffered. Forbes published an article entitled "Americans Sit More Than Any Time in History and It's Literally Killing Us". Need I say more? Probably not, but I will. They found "Sedentary jobs have increased 83% since 1950 according to the American Heart Association."[1] They continue by saying something profound:

> It's not the act of sitting itself that will kill you, but the repercussions of moving too little.

Johns Hopkins found that "physically active jobs now make up less than 20% of the U.S. workforce, down from roughly half of jobs in 1960."[2] Think about it. Let's say you work in a cubicle for eight hours per day, most of it sitting. You drive home, doing what? Sitting in the car. When you get home, what do you want to do? My guess is you sit down and relax. Our natural inclination is to sit around all day, and the results are disastrous.

The Mayo Clinic found that the risks of sitting too much are "increased blood pressure, high blood sugar, excess body fat around the waist, and abnormal cholesterol levels—that make up metabolic syndrome. Too much sitting overall and prolonged periods of sitting also seem to increase the risk of death from cardiovascular disease and cancer."[3]

The decline of active work, leisure, and overall lifestyle has had significant repercussions on our lives. According to the World Health Organization, worldwide obesity has nearly tripled since 1975.[4] They have also found that 39 percent of adults are overweight, while 13 percent would be classified as obese. Obesity can lead to serious physical issues such as cardiovascular disease, diabetes, some forms of cancer, and musculoskeletal disorders.

I do not shed light on these statistics to bring shame or devalue individuals. My goal is to highlight the risks associated with the lack of intentionality when it comes to physical maintenance. There are also other reasons for obesity, such as hormone disorders and the inability to regulate hormones correctly. By no means am I attempting to bring condemnation on anyone. However, stewardship is a serious issue. Stewardship of our bodies, to the best of our abilities, is vital.

Now for the link to those of us who deal with various forms of mental illnesses. The National Institute of Health conducted a study to see if there is in fact an association between obesity and various mental disorders, and they concluded:

> Obesity is associated with an approximately 25% increase in odds of mood and anxiety disorders.[5]

The NIH isn't the only one to find links between an unhealthy lifestyle and mental illness. WHO (the World Health Organization) states another risk associated with obesity and those overweight is "psychological effects."[6] For years, doctors, counselors, and nutritionists have been studying the correlation between mental health and healthy lifestyles and are finding quite a few connections. The Mental Health Foundation states that "the relationship between obesity and mental health problems is complex. Results from a 2010 systematic review found two-way associations between depression and obesity, finding that people who were obese had a 55% increased risk of developing depression over time, whereas people experiencing depression had a 58% increased risk of becoming obese."[7]

All that is to say that your physical health really matters; it's kind of a big deal. If you do not pay attention to the physical, prepare for the mind to be triggered. The question is, WHAT aspects of health matter the most in best caring for and nurturing mental health? I'm so glad you asked.

The Three Horsemen of Fitness

I've entitled this section "The Three Horsemen of Fitness" for the sole purpose of it sounding like the subplot for a Michael Bay movie. Just picture massive explosions as John Cena, Terry Crews, and The Rock gallop along on wild stallions. Three horsemen and fitness conquering triggers of invisible illness.

Three areas of physical health, with some focus and discipline, can help mitigate physical mental-illness triggers. This is not an all-inclusive list by any means, but the three we will discuss are often avoided and simple, yet not easy, to implement. Those three areas are nutrition, sleep, and exercise.

Nutrition

If I had a least favorite part of living a healthy lifestyle, proper nutrition would be it. The majority of my extended family hails from the southeastern part of the United States. In that region of the good ol' US of A, food is really good. Like really, really good. The problem is it will also kill you by exploding your heart. My parents and grandparents knew how to throw down in the kitchen with some old-fashioned comfort food. There are very few things on planet earth I enjoy more than chicken-fried steak smothered in country-style gravy. The problem is that one item alone is typically over 1200 calories. Just because something tastes great doesn't mean it's good for you.

For a moment, I want to start with the basics of how nutrition works. Again, as a disclaimer, I am not a nutritionist; I am a pastor who is learning as I go.

We all need fuel to function. Food is that fuel, and it contains units of energy called calories. We all need calories to live. Just as fuel is vital for cars or planes or any method of transportation to operate, so are calories are vital to our function. The issue comes when we have an overabundance of calories. Calories that are not utilized or burned are stored as fat. Specifically, excess calories are mainly stored as triglycerides, which, when stored up, can cause cardiovascular issues. We already discussed the mental-health issues associated with too much weight.

Our foods are broken up into three basic macronutrients— protein, carbohydrates, and fat. We need all three to function, think, and feel our best. There is quite a debate in the health community on the proper balance between the three macronutrients. As a rule, here is the goal;

eat clean calories and stay away from anything processed.

Not all calories, carbs, fats, and proteins are created equal. A Big Mac might be the same caloric intake as salmon with a side of sweet potatoes, but those calories are vastly different. Processed foods usually contain some form of high-fructose corn syrup, saturated fat, polyunsaturated fat, monounsaturated fat, trans fat, or other additives known to cause health complications.

In the '70s and '80s, bodybuilders were known to load up on any and every food source just to reach a caloric surplus, in hopes of bulking up for their high-stress workouts. After extensive study, the health community reached a consensus: not all calories are the same. Nutrients and the lack thereof in our diets matter. Healthline says:

> While bulking, some bodybuilders also tend to eat calorie-dense, nutrient-poor foods,... including sweets, desserts, and fried foods. These foods, especially when eaten as part of a high-calorie diet, can increase markers of inflammation, promote insulin resistance, and raise levels of fat in your blood.[8]

Nutrition matters for your physical well-being, but it also matters for your mental well-being. Eva Selhub, MD, wrote for the *Harvard Health Blog*, investigating the connections between food and mental health and found that "serotonin is a neurotransmitter that helps regulate sleep and appetite, mediate moods, and inhibit pain. Since about 95% of your serotonin is produced in your gastrointestinal tract, and your gastrointestinal tract is lined with a hundred million nerve cells, or neurons, it makes sense that the inner workings of your digestive system don't just help you digest food, but also guide your emotions. What's more, the function of these neurons—and the production of neurotransmitters like serotonin—is highly influenced by the billions of 'good' bacteria that make up your intestinal microbiome. These bacteria play an essential role in your health. They protect the lining of your intestines and ensure they provide a strong barrier against toxins and 'bad' bacteria; they limit inflammation; they improve how well you absorb nutrients from your food, and they activate neural pathways that travel directly between the gut and the brain."[9]

Serotonin is a neurotransmitter (a messenger) in the brain. It is often referred to as the "happy chemical", because it largely "contributes to well-being and happiness."[10]Around 95 percent of the happy chemical is produced in the gastrointestinal tract (path of food), which is lined with nerves. Therefore, what you eat affects your brain and how you feel. Poor nutrition is linked to low production of serotonin, and low serotonin is linked to an increase in the risk of depression.[11]

All that is to say that your nutrition matters. As a rule, according to the CDC and Dietary Guidelines:

A healthy eating pattern includes:

- A variety of vegetables from all of the subgroups—dark green, red and orange, legumes (beans and peas), starchy, and other

- Fruits, especially whole fruits
- Grains, at least half of which are whole grains
- Fat-free or low-fat dairy, including milk, yogurt, cheese, and/or fortified soy beverages
- A variety of protein foods, including seafood, lean meats and poultry, eggs, legumes (beans and peas), and nuts, seeds, and soy products
- Oils

A healthy eating pattern limits:

- Saturated fats and trans fats, added sugars, and sodium
- Added sugars—consume less than 10 percent of calories per day from this source
- Saturated fat—consume less than 10 percent of calories per day from this source
- Sodium—consume less than 2,300 milligrams (mg) per day[12]

So, let's eat healthily. It matters to your body, and it can limit triggers for episodes of invisible illness.

Sleep

As I've shared, my wife and I had a baby in 2019. He was a bit of a runt at nine pounds and five ounces. Don't tell my wife I said that—my life would be in jeopardy. My wife went through over twenty-eight hours of labor before Levi arrive; which means twenty-eight hours wide awake waiting for his arrival. I have never been so tired in my life. That day, I realized how little I had valued and honored sleep in years prior. I had scorned—nay, spat upon—the precious gift of sleep. How careless I was as a single and a young married man. If I could, I would slap young me in the face for abandoning sweet sleep for another game of Madden. What a fool.

We often overlook the importance of rest and sleep to our physical and mental well-being. Sleep is vital to our ability to function. AAA conducted a study a number of years back in which they compared the dangers of drowsy drivers as compared to drunk drivers. They found that "drivers who miss two to three hours of sleep a day more than quadruple their risk of getting in a crash… According to federal regulators, the accident risk from drowsy driving is comparable to driving drunk."[13]

According to the report, sleep is vital to maintaining reaction time and safety while operating a vehicle. The problem is we often live at such a breakneck pace that we neglect our need for sleep. A Forbes article entitled "America The Sleep-Deprived" stated that "In 2013 (the last year measured by Gallup), the average American slept 6.8 hours a night—with 40 percent banking less than six hours. The nation hasn't always been this sleep-deprived: Back in 1910, people slept an average of nine hours per night."[14]

In 1942, 84 percent of Americans netted seven hours or more of sleep, and by 2013, that number had dipped to 59 percent.[15] We aren't sleeping—we are pushing the limit. Life is run, run, run, and our mental and physical health are suffering because of it.

The EHE found that "in sleep-deprived patients, the amygdala, a part of the brain that processes emotion, becomes 'rewired' in a way that reduces our rational response to external events. These individuals have big emotional swings, going from upset to giddy in moments. Sleep deprivation can even create symptoms similar to those of schizophrenia."[16]

One study showed that those who experience chronic insomnia were twenty times more likely to experience a panic disorder and five times more likely to experience depression.[17]

Invisible illness can lead to sleep deprivation, and sleep deprivation can ignite invisible illness. Kendra Cherry says it this way: "Some psychiatric conditions can cause sleep problems, and sleep disturbances can also exacerbate the symptoms of many mental conditions including depression, anxiety, and bipolar disorder."[18] We need to slow down and get some sleep. The NIH recommends that adults get between seven and nine hours of sleep every night for optimal function.[19]

Some other things we can do to improve our sleep are:

- Limit napping
- Establish a nightly routine
- Avoid caffeine or stimulants too close to bedtime
- Turn off our devices[20]

Sleep is vital to our mental and physical health. Let's prioritize it.

Exercise

We all know that exercise is important. On every device we consume media, there is a consistent flood of fad workouts, celebrity-endorsed health products, and pleas for our kids to "Play 60" minutes a day. Working out is something we all know we should probably do more of, just like we know we should probably clean the bathroom grout. It's hard to muster up the will to whip out the brush and get to scrubbin'. It's necessary but not exactly enjoyable.

However, many of us that deal with various invisible illnesses probably don't understand how our lack of exercise contributes to our lack of mental health. The body God designed for us is amazing in how it releases natural hormones and chemicals to keep us balanced. Endorphins are such chemicals. Endorphins are our bodies' natural chemicals, released to reduce stress and pain and help with feeling good overall. Endorphins release positive feelings that are comparable to morphine.[21] Yes, morphine. Ever heard of a runner's high? That high is the release of endorphins causing a feeling of euphoria.

Here are some activities that can release endorphins:

- Biking
- Dancing
- Gardening
- Golf (walking instead of using the cart)
- Housework, especially sweeping, mopping, or vacuuming

- Jogging at a moderate pace
- Low-impact aerobics
- Tennis
- Swimming
- Walking
- Yard work, especially mowing or raking
- Yoga[22]

WebMD states, "Research has shown that exercise is an effective but often underused treatment for mild to moderate depression. In addition, exercise outside (with the appropriate sun protection) can help boost levels of vitamin D and your mood."[23]

They continue by highlighting some other benefits of consistent physical exertion: a reduction in stress, warding off anxiety and feelings of depression, boosting self-esteem, and improving sleep. Those seem like some solid benefits. Here is the thing—you don't have to become Crossfit Kelly in order to reap benefits. Studies show that even ten minutes a day of exercise can help start the endorphin-releasing process.[24]

The point is this: get moving. Whatever your lifestyle looks like right now, step it up a notch. A lack of physical activity is a trigger, so get to exercising.

If we lack the intentionality to manage and maintain our bodies, our minds begin to decline. For those of us who deal with varying mental illnesses, we cannot neglect the physical.

Remember, triggers set things off. So why not eliminate as many triggers as possible? Take care of your body. Clean up your diet, watch fewer episodes before bed, hit the hay at a reasonable hour, and go for a walk. Your body is a temple, and you've only been given one. Honor God with your body.

CHAPTER 5

RELATIONAL TRIGGERS

> *No road is long with good company.*
> *—Turkish Proverb*

In 1787, the Quakers, a religious pacifist group, conducted an experiment in hopes of rehabilitating hardened criminals. They were inspired by the thought of setting inmates free from the "perversion" of society and spurring individuals on to spiritual awakening. The experiment- solitary confinement. The goal was not to torture—it was to rehabilitate, it was ecstasy, to reach a sort of nirvana. Yet, the experiment, started at Walnut Street Jail in Philadelphia, serves as proof of what God stated thousands of years prior: "It is not good for man to be alone" (Genesis 2:18).

As a clinical psychiatrist, majoring in the study of the effects of those isolated in prison, Stuart Grassian explains, "There was a belief that you could put a prisoner in his solitary cell, freed from the evil influences of modern society… and they would become like a monk in a monastic cell, free to come close to God and to their own inner being, and they would naturally heal from the evils of the outside society.… It was a noble experiment that was an absolute catastrophe."[1]

Jason M. Breslow, in an article for *Frontline*, states, "When corrections officials talk about solitary confinement, they describe it as the prison within the prison."[2]

Harry Harlow of the University of Wisconsin conducted a now infamous study in which he placed rhesus monkeys in what was nicknamed "the pit of despair". This solitary pit was shaped like an upside-down obelisk. The sides were slick, and escaping the pit was nearly impossible. After observing these monkeys only a few days, Harlow observed that "most subjects typically assume a hunched position in a corner of the bottom of the apparatus. One might presume at this point that they find their situation to be hopeless." He found that prolonged periods of isolation led the monkeys to be "given to staring blankly and rocking in place for long periods, circling their cages repetitively, and mutilating themselves.… Twelve months of isolation almost obliterated the animals socially."[3]

For obvious reasons, tests like these have not been conducted on humans, but what have been calculated are the long-term effects of solitary confinement.

Psychologist Craig Haney conducted a study in 2003 at Pelican Bay. Haney interviewed one hundred random inmates held in solitary and found that the overwhelming majority reported increased anxiety, irrational anger and irritability, confusion in their thought processes, and sensitivity to external stimulants. "Some 70 percent felt themselves to be on the verge of a nervous breakdown, about 40 percent experienced hallucinations, and just under a third reported suicidal thoughts."[4]

Former Harvard Medical School Faculty Stuart Grassian, in interviewing countless inmates who have endured solitary confinement, found that around one-third of solitary inmates were "actively psychotic and/or acutely suicidal."[5]

Solitary confinement is obviously an extreme measure of isolation, but the moral of the story is this: people were designed for people. We were designed to know and be known, to love and be loved, to hold and be held. Community is vital. Within the United States, there has been an unhealthy trend toward individualism for decades, and we are reaping detrimental results from it.

Me or Us?

For most of history, humanity has primarily been tribal, meaning the needs of the whole outweigh the needs of the one. The individual came second; the needs of the community came first. The concept of community priority is called collectivism, while cultures that prioritize the individual subscribe to individualism. While some aspects of both are beneficial, when played out over decades, we have seen the extremes of individualism produce negative results in the West.

Though the term *individualism* was not coined until the nineteenth century in France, the ideologies behind individualism are centuries old. We get hints of individualistic thinking as far back as the fifth century BCE in ancient Indian and Chinese traditions. Socrates believed and taught that various types of wisdom could not be shared from one human to another, but they must be obtained through individual life experience. Certain truths could not be transferred but were individualistic. Christianity spread from an Eastern tribal culture to the culture of the West, which was largely shaped by Athenian teaching and ideologies. With that blend, alongside the core Christian tenets of personal conversion and personal relationship with the Son of God, societies began to apply and value, above all else, personal experience and individual liberty.

Personal liberty in and of itself is of the utmost importance when in conjunction with corporate care, but it makes a terrible idol. Individualism, in the sense of taking responsibility for one's life and becoming the best version of oneself to become a net positive to society, is a completely Christian notion. But the idea that our individuality and fulfillment should be our chief concern, the rest of humanity be damned, comes from hell. I am not condemning the whole concept of individualism. Much of the impetus behind the birth of America was the belief that individual liberty mattered. Humans were not destined to live in poverty or subservience to others who may be deemed higher up in the societal castes. Individuals matter. Each is made in the image and likeness of God. Individuals are worth fighting for and dying for. I'm not arguing for some sort of socialistic thinking; on the contrary, socialistic societies invariably devolve into cannibalizing the poor and hurting.

Yet, played to its unhealthy extreme, the prioritizing of individual liberty has evolved from a fight for "certain inalienable rights" for all, to "my rights are all that matter." The evolution from "all men are created equal" to a self-sustaining island of individualism is detrimental to the individual and society.

We see through history the morphing of society from a "what's-best-for-the-rest" mentality to a "what's-in-it-for-me" cry. The focus on individual freedom is good and right, yet the overextension of individuality leading to a disregard of others has culminated in many experiencing loneliness and despair. Over time, we are becoming more and more and more alone.

Independent and alone.

Individual and lonely.

Free and depressed.

Freedom is a God idea; liberty was authored in the mind of the Creator. Yet, as is typical, humans have taken a God idea to its unhealthy extreme. The idea we are exploring in this chapter is this: a lack of healthy relationships is a trigger for poor mental health.

Me, Myself, and I

In the past century, modern Western culture has become more and more isolated. Simply look at the transformation of suburban architecture and the cultural leanings are obvious. American homes went from having large, pronounced front porches to removing front porches in favor of large backyards. This trend is clear: privacy is of more value than hospitality. How often do neighbors get home, pull straight into the garage, shut the door, and never speak with one another?

With the increased development of technology, we live in a contradictory world. We are more connected than we have ever been, yet we are more isolated than we have ever been.

My parents have always been the couple that teenagers adore. They were kids' pastors and youth pastors for the majority of my childhood and have become parents to countless adolescent youngsters. After all of their kids moved out, they couldn't help themselves—they opened their home to two high school exchange students. A few years ago, my wife and I were having dinner with my parents and their two students. Over the course of three or so hours, we laughed, made inappropriate jokes, reveled in our sarcasm, and noticed that neither student (who spoke fine English) spoke to us or each other for the entire evening. They looked at their phones.

The. Entire. Time.

They were playing a game. They were playing the same game, against each other, together, with zero dialogue. They sat less than a foot away from one another, playing the same game with no trash talk. No trash talk? What kind of nonsense is that? How boring.

Yet, this is not a specific generation's problem. This heightened focus on technology at the expense of interpersonal relationships is not simply the defect of Millennials or Gen Z. This is a societal issue. I frequently catch both of my boomer parents on the couch, accompanied by a few millennials, ALL on their phones as they binge-watch the latest Netflix special. We are addicted to screens. Now, one screen isn't enough. We need the TV on, and the latest iPhone tucked neatly beside our laptop, all simultaneously spitting out information that gives us the illusion of community. Many of us actually believe our followers on Instagram or our Facebook friends equate with real-life relationships. The problem is, in reality, we are becoming more and more isolated, and it is stunting our spiritual, mental, and physical growth.

We will discuss the benefits and drawbacks of social media in a later chapter—that is not our focus here. But let me say this: many of us are substituting real, living, breathing relationships for "connections" on screens. Social media is a cheap imitation of community. Community is what our souls long for, and when deprived of community, our mental health suffers.

Vast studies have been conducted on the effect community has on mental health. The bottom line is that the stronger your relationships and community, the better your mental health. The Mental Health Foundation says; "People who are more socially connected to family, friends, or their community are happier, physically healthier, and live longer, with fewer mental health problems than people who are less well connected." They continue to say; "Extensive evidence shows that having good-quality relationships can help us to live longer and happier lives with fewer mental health problems. Having close, positive relationships can give us a purpose and sense of belonging."[6]

Harvard conducted a study in 1936 with 724 participants. The goal of the study was to determine the answer to the age-old question: What makes humans happy? A plethora of metrics was taken into account, including IQ, social life, and physical and psychosocial makeup. The conclusions of the survey were published in the book *Triumphs of Experience*. The findings showed that the biggest determining factor of happiness and health was healthy relationships.[7]

Not wealth.

Not fame.

Not beauty.

Not social standing.

It was relationships. It was knowing others and being known by others.

However, there is a problem. Anyone who has ever dealt with invisible illness knows that one of its first side effects is isolation.

We draw away.

We hide.

We insulate.

Isolation triggers mental illness and mental illness triggers isolation. It's a catch-22, a vicious cycle. How to conquer one without the ramifications of the other? How do we nurture life-giving relationships when our mind is screaming, "HIDE!"? The answer, like most answers to these types of questions, is simple but not easy. The answer is like Nike.

Just. Do. It.

On your good days, force yourself to pour into what matters—people.

Relationships—A God Idea

Earlier in this chapter, I made a passing reference to the first mention in Scripture of the imperative of human relationships. Let's dive deeper into this.

God creates the universe in stages, pausing briefly after each stage to observe that "it was good."

Skies—good.

Animals—good.

Night and day—good.

Humanity—very good.

But then God observes something that does not reflect Him. He observes something in nature that does not reveal itself in the Godhead. He observes isolation. Man is alone.

God in and of Himself exudes perfect community. Father, Son, and Holy Spirit eternally reign in the perfect manifestation of community. So united is their being that the three are one, and the one is three. Humanity, made in the image and likeness of God, is designed to function best within the context of community. God steps back from every step of creation and declares, "it is good", except for seeing man alone, which He observes is "not good."

So, God fixes that issue. Why? Because humanity is not designed by the Designer to operate independently from other image bearers.

Isolated individualism is not within the perfect design of humanity. I need you, and you need me. God has designed us to be independent—meaning we have the capacity for free will, and interdependent—meaning there will be glitches in the software when we are isolated.

PROVERBS 17:17 NIV

"A FRIEND LOVES
AT ALL TIMES,
AND A BROTHER
IS BORN FOR
A TIME OF
ADVERSITY."

Scripture is replete with references to the importance of living in community. Here are a few examples:

> A friend loves at all times,
> and a brother is born for a time of adversity.
> (Proverbs 17:17)

> How good and pleasant it is
> when God's people live together in unity!
> It is like precious oil poured on the head,
> running down on the beard,
> running down on Aaron's beard,
> down on the collar of his robe. (Psalm 133:1-2)

> Two are better than one,
> because they have a good return for their labor:
> If either of them falls down,
> one can help the other up.
> But pity anyone who falls
> and has no one to help them up.
> Also, if two lie down together, they will keep warm.
> But how can one keep warm alone?
> Though one may be overpowered,
> two can defend themselves.
> A cord of three strands is not quickly broken.
> (Ecclesiastes 4:9-12)

We must fight for community. I'm well aware that that statement feels like an oxymoron. Fight for community? Shouldn't community just be natural? Shouldn't community just be chemistry based? In short, no. No relationship worth its salt is 100 percent organic. Relationships that stand the test of time are built with intentionality.

Our society worships the idols of convenience and comfort, which is why so many settle for isolation. Isolation is easy; community is difficult. Yet isolation is toxic, and community is life giving.

Back to the biggest issue with all of this stuff: one of the first reactions of those suffering from invisible illness is shrinking into isolation. If this is you, you're in good company. Remember Elijah? Remember what happens when he is threatened by Jezebel? He flees, leaves his crew behind, and goes it alone. The result is a powerful, spirit-filled man of God begging the Creator to end his life.

Long-term isolation breeds death. Period.

Practical Application

Hopefully, at this point, you understand how bad isolation is for you mentally, physically, psychologically. If not, I'll say it again. Isolation is *really* bad.

Like the Sacramento Kings bad.
The Jacksonville Jaguars bad.
Don't do it.

Again, I know that is easier said than done. I am a self-proclaimed extroverted introvert. I love people in doses, but I really love my time alone. People are amazing, but they drain the life out of me. As a pastor, a massive part of my job is working rooms and having tons of personal conversations. The problem is all of that is exhausting, and oftentimes my knee-jerk reaction is to isolate for long periods of time, claiming I am "recharging."

Now, to a degree, that is true. I do need to recharge alone. You can only pour out what you have. If you are always pouring out and never refilling, you will burn out. It's not a matter of if, it's a matter of when. But I tend to almost always lean into isolation rather than community, which is incredibly unhealthy. So, I have to be intentional about forcing myself to develop community. There will be a day when I will need my community—my circle—to lean on.

Gospel Community

One of my favorite peeks into the life of Jesus is found in Mark 2. Jesus has just begun His ministry teaching in the synagogues and astounding the religious elite with His authority and grasp of Old Testament theology. His authority in the Scriptures extends to His healing of the physically ill and demonized. Scripture records that Jesus's renown has begun to spread all across Judea.

Jesus, the carpenter and healer.

In Mark 2, Jesus returns to Capernaum, welcomed by multitudes of hurting, sick, and broken people. He posts up in a home and begins to teach.

As He teaches, a paralyzed man finds himself at one of the meetings. This man has no hope of physical revitalization, barring an act of divine intervention. Here is what is vital to note: he is only in the proximity of a miracle because he has four friends who care enough to carry him to the Messiah. He can't heal himself, carry himself, or fix himself. He needs community.

I haven't lived on this planet for that long, but what I have seen is this: there are days when you need to be carried, and days you will be carrying others. We are wired for it.

Paul says this:

> Bear one another's burdens, and so fulfill the law of Christ. (Galatians 6:2)

We are designed to bear one another's burdens and have our burdens carried. That takes intentionality and proximity. So, here are three practical steps to eliminate the isolation trigger in your life:

1. Invest in others today

Simply put, invest in other people. Think of relationships as a bank—there are deposits and withdrawals. You can only withdraw what you deposit, or you overdraw. Often, the difficult relationships in our lives have to do with a poor balance of withdrawals and deposits. Solomon states this:

> A man *who has* friends must himself be friendly,

But there is a friend *who* sticks closer than a brother.
(Proverbs 18:24)

If you find yourself lacking friends, maybe you haven't shown yourself friendly. Don't be a taker all the time.

Give.
Invest in others.
Deposit now, withdraw later.

2. Check on people when you don't need anything

We all know the feeling of seeing a phone call, a text, or an email, knowing that there is an "ask" coming. Don't be that friend. Be a no-agenda friend.

I remember taking a pastor friend of mine to lunch for the first time. At the time, I was the youth pastor at a small church, and my friend had a large, influential youth ministry with national notoriety. This guy is a rock star in all things youth ministry. As we sat down eating our Chick-fil-A and enjoying calorie-dense milkshakes, he interrupted the moment and got right to the point.

"So, what do you need?"

My friend was so used to people befriending him solely for his resources, help, or influence that the concept of a no-strings-attached lunch seemed foreign. When I informed him there was no agenda—no "ask"—that I just wanted to be friends, the look of shock on his face broke my heart.

From that day forward, we continued to check up on each other frequently. Some days, I carried him; other days, he carried me. Motives kill relationships. Love people for the sake of loving people and check on your friends.

3. Don't be afraid to cry out for help

Here is the thing—you can't do this one if you haven't done the other two. Some of us need to focus on the other two really badly. Some of us (I'm looking at you, Pastor) need to get better at this.

Admittedly, I'm bad at crying out for help. I'm a three on the enneagram. I'm an achiever, go-getter, doer, accomplisher to the max. I have a hard time calling in other people to help. I don't even work out with a spotter—which, by the way, is stupid.

Calling in others to help, especially in the realm of mental illness, is really difficult for me. Yet, I have been intentional in inviting others into the fight, and it has made all the difference in the world. Now I'm not bearing this on my own. I have others praying for me, encouraging me, texting me at random times, reminding me of who God has called me to be. You know what that is? It's others carrying my burdens.

People can't fight for you if you don't tell them there is a fight.

I've learned that people are not as psychic as we think. They are not mind readers, and those of us who have dealt with chronic invisible illness for extended times are *really good* at hiding what is bombarding our minds. We have to invite others into the battle—invite them into the fight.

In Exodus 17, there is a story about the Israelite army, led by Joshua, locked in battle with the Amalekites. Moses, the leader, stands atop a hill with his arms outstretched, raising the staff of God. When his arms are raised, the Israelites inch closer to victory; as his arms droop, they lose ground. So, Aaron and Hur climb the hill and hold up Moses's arms to ensure victory. The victory comes not as the result of one man's bravado and pure internal fortitude, but because a few friends hold up the arms of their leader.

God is to be glorified from the victories we experience and from the lives that we live, yet we cannot do it alone. Victory is not accomplished alone. Victory is not achieved through rugged individualism. We are the Body of Christ, all connected and interconnected. I need you, and you need me. We must seek out community and fight to know and be known. Isolation is a trigger for mental illness. Resist the pull of isolation and endeavor to bear others' burdens and have yours borne by others.

CHAPTER 6

SPIRITUAL TRIGGERS

> *While God allows sickness and we can, thankfully, grow from it, nevertheless, it is inherently evil, and we should do everything we can to get well.*
>
> —J. P. Moreland, *Finding Quiet*

Just as there are natural triggers in the realms of our physical upkeep and maintaining and investing in our relationships, there are spiritual triggers as well. To hammer this point home—beat a dead horse, scream it till the cows come home—pick your confusing analogy, we as humans are one complete being made up of three unique parts: spirit, soul, and body. Each aspect affects the others. The soul affects the spirit; the spirit affects the soul; the body affects the other two. They all are related to one another. Spiritual things are not just spiritual things.

Twenty-first-century culture is largely influenced by neo-Gnostic ideas that seek to compartmentalize the human experience. Gnosticism reveals itself in a variety of breeds but can best be summarized as the belief that anything spiritual is good and right, and anything natural is wicked and evil. Gnostic-thinking individuals subscribe to the idea that the spiritual has no effect on the natural, and the natural has no effect on the spiritual. We are completely compartmentalized beings, and what we do with our bodies brings no consequence in the eternal. The church fathers were constantly battling against Gnostic thinking sneaking into the hearts and minds of early followers of Jesus. John pens his first epistle largely calling out the Gnostic heresies that were perverting the doctrine of fresh converts.

Many unknowingly subscribe to twenty-first-century Gnosticism by pursuing hedonism above all else, while dabbling in various forms of spiritual enlightenment. This ideology leads to dualistic lifestyles both outside the confines of the faith community and within it. Christ followers are being wooed by a subtle form of compartmentalizing Gnosticism. Within the Church, those who have bought into this heresy live like hell Monday through Saturday, then repent, confess, and seek out special revelation on Sunday, only to repeat the same cycle over and over again. It's a death-producing, Satan-inspired farce.

The idea that we can compartmentalize the core aspects of what makes us human and believe there are no long-term repercussions is heretical and dangerous. The spiritual has vast consequences on the physical, which includes our mental states.

Two Culprits

Through Scripture, we find spiritual triggers that affect us mentally and physically. For our purposes here, I have grouped them into two main spiritual triggers. These two triggers encompass many factors and choices and, interestingly enough, influence each other.

Sin

Let's jump right into the deep end here and discuss the ramifications of sin. Much of Western society would scoff at sin, and the very idea of sin would be abhorrent. The culture we are steeped in doesn't subscribe to objective truth. What's right for you isn't right for me, and vice versa. We're told that we live in a grey world; black and white do not exist.

Today's culture is largely shaped by postmodernism, which began to gain traction in the twentieth century. Postmodernism seeks to tear down absolutes and shuns traditional assumptions about morality, truth, and objective reality. This way of thinking found a ready audience in the increasingly godless society of the twentieth-century and continues to have a hold in our century. What are the results of this way of thinking? Graham Johnson details some tenets of the postmodernist:

1. They're reacting to modernity and its tenets
2. They reject objective truth
3. They're skeptical and suspicious of authority
4. They're like missing persons in search of a self and identity
5. They've blurred morality and are into whatever's expedient
6. They continue to search for the transcendent
7. They're living in a media world unlike any other
8. They'll engage in a knowing smirk
9. They're on a quest for community
10. They live in a very material world[1]

This is the mindset many of us subconsciously cling to and employ in our daily lives. The idea of sin is offensive to those who do not believe in objective truth. Yet, God, being a loving, caring Father as well as the Designer of all things material and immaterial, wants our best and knows how we best function. Regardless of what postmodernism and 21st culture might suggest, there is right and wrong.

Good and evil.
Truth and falsehood.
Holiness and sinfulness.
Humanity was not designed to operate with the defilement of sin.

Sin has become a vague concept that for many is hard to define. In Scripture, the definition of *sin* is simple: it means "to miss the mark." The mark—the goal, our aim—should be to be as Christlike as possible. Two portions of Scripture give us a clear glimpse into what Christlikeness looks like:

> But the fruit of the Spirit is love, joy, peace, forbearance, kindness, goodness, faithfulness, gentleness, and self-control. Against such things there is no law. (Galatians 5:22–23 NIV)

> Love is patient, love is kind. It does not envy, it does not boast, it is not proud. It does not dishonor others, it is not self-seeking, it is not easily angered; it keeps no record of wrongs. Love does not delight in evil but rejoices with the truth. It always protects, always trusts, always hopes, always perseveres. Love never fails. (1 Corinthians 13:4–8 NIV)

These portions of Scripture detail some of the characteristics of Jesus. They detail the mark we should all aim to hit. The original intent of our humanity is to exude all of these godly characteristics, thus glorifying God. They describe the beauty of Jesus.

To sin is to miss the mark—to fail to reflect Christlikeness. Sin has horrific results for us in our mental, physical, and spiritual well-being.

David, one of the heroes of Scripture, clearly dealt with a variety of mental struggles, as we have discussed. He is called a man after God's own heart, yet he had some sketchy patches in his life.

Kings customarily led their armies into battle, protecting the sovereignty of the nations they led and expanding the borders of their rule. King David often led his army into battle but on some occasions opted for comfort instead. In Second Samuel 11, we find King David abdicating his role as commander-in-chief of Israel's army preferring to stay home and gaze over the splendor of his kingdom from the roof of his palace in Jerusalem. At this point in his life, it's apparent he did not hold the customs of kingship in high regard. David chooses the easy path. The easy path leads his eyes to wander past the splendor of *what* he is called to lead and onto a *who*. A *who* who is bathing. A *who* who is named Bathsheba.

At that moment, David's desire for Bathsheba outweighs his love for the law of God. A child is conceived out of the sin that David commits. Yet, David doesn't stop at adultery. When learning of the child-to-be, and after numerous attempts to cover up his affair, he has Bathsheba's husband, Uriah the Hittite, murdered.

David—man after God's own heart—now an adulterous murderer.

David is confronted by the prophet Nathan and is quick to repent, as we read in one of the most famous prayers in Scripture, Psalm 51. There is a particular line that always catches my attention:

> Restore to me the joy of Your salvation
> and grant me a willing spirit, to sustain me. (Psalm
> 51:12 NIV)

Let's piece together this prayer from the original Hebrew. The word "restore" is the Hebrew word *shuv, meaning* "to turn back, return." "Joy" is the word *sason*, meaning "exultation", "rejoicing." "Of Your salvation" is *yesha*, meaning "deliverance", "rescue", "salvation", "safety", "welfare."

David's prayer is, "God, return to me the ability to rejoice and exalt in what You've done. I've lost it."

David, the naked dancer, no longer danced—no longer had *sason*.

Sin stole his *sason*.
Sin saps joy.
Sin causes celebration to seem uninviting.
Exaltation seems worthless.

I've experienced this firsthand. As someone who has depressive inclinations, when I have engaged in blatant, unrepentant sin, my joy, peace, and happiness have been sapped. I dealt with a porn addiction for years. I knew it wasn't God's best, but I was addicted. I couldn't seem to stop. Part of the beauty of our Messiah is His love for us regardless of how broken we are when we come to Him. Another part of His beauty is His adamance that we not stay that way. I would frequently feel the prompting of the Holy Spirit to change, to abandon my sin. This tug is called conviction, the sting of God saying, "This isn't best."

Conviction pleads with us to repent and change and is birthed out of a call to be all God has designed us to be.
Condemnation may poke at the same sin, yet it offers no hope for change.

Condemnation is from Satan.
Conviction is from God.

I would feel conviction for my sin, and, when I ignored it, my sin produced shame and guilt, and was a trigger for depressive episodes.

As a pastor now, I frequently discuss mental illness with individuals. After hearing the individual's story, life experiences, and family history, in an attempt to understand a sketch of their mental well-being, I often ask, "Are you living in unrepentant sin?" I ask this not out of condemnation but out of compassion. I want to do my best to help the individual guard against the consequences attached to sin.

Here is the thing with sin: we are all guilty.

> For all have sinned and fall short of the glory of God. (Romans 3:23 NIV)

As it is written:

> "None is righteous, no, not one;
>   no one understands;

no one seeks for God." (Romans 3:10–11 ESV)

The question is not:

"Am I a sinner?"

The questions we must ask are:

"Have I turned from my sin?"
"Have I submitted my sin to Jesus?"
"Am I pursuing the life *HE* has for me?"

We are all jacked up. We are all broken. We all need healing. No matter where you are on the spectrum of sin, all humanity stands on a level playing field before the cross. The cross is the great equalizer of man. The key is realizing our brokenness and refusing to acquiesce to it. The consequences of sin are clear in Scripture:

For the wages of sin is death; but the gift of God is eternal life through Jesus Christ our Lord. (Romans 6:23 *KJV*)

Sin produces relational death, physical death, mental death, spiritual death, and eternal death. Run from sin. For those of us who deal with invisible illness, living in sin is a trigger.

We are designed to live sin free, in the light, in a tight-knit relationship with our Creator. Maybe the reason some of us continue to experience mental instability is that we have yet to embrace repentance, and yield the whole of our lives to the

Lordship of Jesus. To repent simply means to be walking in one direction, then stop, turn, and walk in the opposite direction. If you are engaging in sin, you need to repent, turn to God, and pursue the righteousness of Christ.

Sin kills.
Sin infects.
Sin saps joy and peace.
Sin accomplishes those things because sin separates us from God.

Humanity at its core was fashioned to live in perfect intimacy with its Designer. Genesis details Adam and Eve walking in the cool of the day with God.

Sin broke that.
Sin separated them.
Sin brought shame.
Sin brought distance.

And sin continues to break, to separate, and to bring shame and distance from God. This is massively problematic, because distance from God is our second spiritual trigger for invisible illness.

"THE CHIEF END OF MAN IS TO GLORIFY GOD AND ENJOY HIM FOREVER."

-THE WESTMINSTER SHORTER CATESCHISM

Distance from God

We have an old-fashioned catch-22 here. Sin causes separation from God, and separation from God leads to sin. Humans experience a void in purpose when not in proximity to the Creator. We are relational by nature, made in the image of a relational being.

The Westminster Shorter Catechism famously describes the purpose of man, stating, "The chief end of man is to glorify God and enjoy Him forever."[2] How beautiful is that? To reflect glory to God and enjoy Him. Enjoyment comes from proximity. We were designed to be close to God, and God desires to come close. One of the most attractive and unique facets of Christianity is the nature of an omniscient, omnipotent Being who lays down immortality and embraces mortality. The Creator wears the garments of skin and bones. Our Kinsman Redeemer, Jesus, God made flesh, God who desires intimacy with an oft-rebellious creation.

Wired into the fiber of our beings is this desire for the eternal, for the *more*. Solomon pens Ecclesiastes 3:11, declaring, "He has put eternity into man's heart." There is a longing, a deep, innate sense of knowing that there is more. There are eternal things. "This" is not all there is. That's because this, the temporal, is not what we were created for. We are eternal beings cloaked in temporal bodies that will one day be stripped away, as we step into eternity. The deep desire for the unseen can only be fulfilled in a vibrant relationship with Jesus. We have been given access to approach the throne of the

Almighty by the finished work of the cross through the Holy Spirit. The writer of Hebrews implores us to "approach God's throne of grace with confidence, so that we may receive mercy and find grace to help us in our time of need."

When submitted to the Lordship of Christ, the Father sees us through the lens of a bloodstained cross. We have a righteousness that is not our own. Paul writes to the church in Corinth that "God made Him who had no sin to be sin for us, so that in Him we might become the righteousness of God."

All of this is simply to say that proximity to God is possible and the chief aim of the Christian. When we are distant, when we refuse to use the access we have been given, we do not operate at peak efficiency. You and I were designed to be close to God. When we are distant, mental illness can be triggered. Our mental state isn't right when we are far off. God doesn't desire separation and didn't program distance into us. He wants us to be close.

> Draw near to God and He will draw near to you. (James 4:8 KJV)

> Then you will call upon Me and go and pray to Me, and I will listen to you. And you will seek Me and find Me, when you search for Me with all your heart. (Jeremiah 29:12–13 KJV)

God gives us the ability to determine proximity. The ball is in our court. Jesus did the heavy lifting by bearing the weight of sin and shame of mankind. The Holy Spirit enlightens our hearts to give us the ability to respond to the Gospel. We get to decide how close we want to live to the God of the universe.

Drawing near is simple. Let's discuss how we draw near:

1. Repent

We dealt with this already in detail, but the life of a Christ follower is a life of consistent repentance and consistent self-diagnosis. David was the man after God's own heart, not because of his perfection, but because he was quick to repent. I've heard it said that the closer we are to Jesus, the less we sin, but the more aware we are of our sin. When the Holy Spirit makes you aware, be quick to repent.

2. Be soaked in Scripture

The Bible is the infallible Word of God. Read, memorize, and meditate on Scripture, and allow Scripture to read you. We must be in Scripture daily, allowing the Spirit of God to speak to us and change us from the Word of God. Paul drops the mic with this:

> All Scripture is God-breathed and is useful for teaching, rebuking, correcting, and training in righteousness, so that the servant of God may be thoroughly equipped for every good work. (2 Timothy 3:16–17 NIV)

3. Pray

God still speaks and wants to speak to you. Prayer is two-way communication with God. Oftentimes, we misconstrue the idea of prayer. We believe the best prayer is recited in King James English, with religious niceties fashioned in long diatribes, seamed together in perfect doctrinal congruity.

Nope.

Prayer is being real and honest with God. Smith Wigglesworth said something that changed my prayer life:

> I don't often spend more than half an hour in prayer at one time, but I never go more than a half an hour without praying.[3]

Be in constant communication with God, and you will begin to experience intimacy with the Father.

4. Worship

Worship, in the life of the believer, tethers us to the eternal. Worship never ceases in heaven. Look at this scene in the book of Revelation.

> Day and night they never stop saying:
> "Holy, holy, holy
> is the Lord God Almighty, who was, and is, and is to come." (Revelation 4:8 NIV)

Then I heard every creature in heaven and on earth and under the earth and on the sea, and all that is in them, saying:

"To Him who sits on the throne and to the Lamb be praise and honor and glory and power, for ever and ever!"

The four living creatures said, "Amen," and the elders fell down and worshiped. (Revelation 5:13–14 NIV)

After this I looked, and behold, a great multitude that no one could number, from every nation, from all tribes and peoples and languages, standing before the throne and before the Lamb, clothed in white robes, with palm branches in their hands, and crying out with a loud voice, "Salvation belongs to our God who sits on the throne, and to the Lamb!" And all the angels were standing around the throne and around the elders and the four living creatures, and they fell on their faces before the throne and worshiped God. (Revelation 7:9–11 ESV)

The scene in heaven revolves around complete worship and surrender. All the heavenly beings never cease to lift their voices to sing and declare the majesty of King Jesus.

Worship is not simply a time of singing while in the corporate gathering of the church. Worship is to be a way of life for followers of Jesus. We must shut the door and plan time to sing and declare the worthiness, holiness, and grandeur of our King.

Worship shifts atmospheres and accomplishes the highest purpose of our lives: to glorify God and enjoy Him forever.

5. Intentional Community

Lastly, let's briefly touch on intentional community as it relates to avoiding spiritual triggers of invisible illness. We spent an entire chapter on the need for healthy relationships, but this is particularly vital in speaking to spiritual well-being and proximity to God. We cannot grow closer to the Creator in isolation. God has designed us to be a part of a life-giving Body of believers called the Church. The word used for the "Church" in Scripture is the Greek word *ekklesia*, which simply means "*an assembly, a congregation*". The Church is not a building or event; the Church is identified as the gathering of Christ followers. Simply put, we must be in godly community. God has designed us to spur one another on in good works. Having a like-minded, Christ-seeking community around us gives us accountability, healing, protection, direction, camaraderie, and encouragement, to name a few things.

Not embracing intentionality in our spiritual health can be a trigger for our invisible illness. We must be quick to turn from sin and pursue closeness to Jesus with every fiber of our being. We are spiritual beings temporarily housed in vessels of clay; let's not neglect our regenerated nature in an attempt to satisfy temporal desires. There is more to life than what we can see. In pursuit of becoming who we were designed to be as prescribed by the Designer, we mitigate spiritual triggers.

PART THREE: HEALING

PART 3

HEALING

> *Beloved, I pray that in all respects you may prosper and be in good health, just as your soul prospers.*
>
> —3 John 2

Well, friends, we are rounding third base here, as we step into our final section: healing. We have discussed where mental illnesses may come from and what they may look like. We have conversed on a few triggers and how best to steward life in an effort to mitigate our experiences with invisible illness. Now, let's talk about how to begin a healing process.

Healing is a loaded word when used in reference to mental health. The life of the Christ-follower is often a supernatural balancing act. Our life is not a life of perfection and constant bliss; trials, hardships, and seasons of difficulty are inevitable. Yet, through the lows of life, peace is our inheritance. Scripture declares:

> And the peace of God, which surpasses all understanding, will guard your hearts and your minds in Christ Jesus. (Philippians 4:7 ESV)

A peace that defies logic is a part of the provision of the finished work of the cross. You and I do not have to settle for chaos and confusion. Peace is our portion.

Life will not be perfect; there may be seasons of intense mental illness that we do not understand. Yet, in difficulty, we praise God and declare that, even in the midst of not seeing peace, peace is ours.

Healing is possible. Rarely does healing come on our timetable, but it is our responsibility to be good stewards of what God has given us. God blesses good stewardship.

In our final section, let's examine some ways we can progress toward healing—how we can steward our lives well and give God glory through the process.

CHAPTER 7

THOUGHT FACTORY

> *We demolish arguments and every pretension that sets itself up against the knowledge of God, and we take captive every thought to make it obedient to Christ.*
>
> *2 Corinthians 10:5*

Have you ever thought how crazy it is that we have the ability to think? We can think whatever we want whenever we want, and those thoughts can lead to other thoughts that just run wild. We can daydream about being astronauts or NBA stars or the best underwater basket weavers on the planet or nomadic journalists who capture the wonders of the world for *National Geographic*. Thoughts are often the vehicle to propel our hopes and dreams, helping us navigate the expanse of what is possible.

The ability to think is pretty amazing.

The problem is, thoughts tend to run amok. Thoughts can be a bit unruly; they behave more like waves of the sea than a boat directed and controlled by a rudder.

When directed positively, thoughts are amazing, housing incredible power. But those same thoughts have the ability to wreak havoc on our mental health. Thoughts are not an innocent, feeble phenomenon; they have the power to cripple us. A well-managed thought life is vital to reaching optimum mental health and then maintaining a life marked by mental stability.

Scripture heralds the importance of thought life.

> For as he thinks in his heart, so *is* he. (Proverbs 23:7 KJV, emphasis mine)

King Solomon, world renowned for his divine wisdom, penned this verse, speaking to a reality that many of us do not understand in full.

"As he thinks in his heart, so *is* he."

You've heard the saying, "You are what you eat." A more incisive saying would be, "You are what y ou think." Henry Ford famously said, "Whether you think you can or you think you can't—you're right." Thinking is powerful. It shapes our concepts of reality and often defines the limits of what we will accomplish. This is why Scripture has quite a bit to say on our thought life.

God's Thoughts on Thinking

Throughout Scripture, we see that God Himself has thoughts. God thinks. Humanity, made in His image and likeness, also thinks. The fact that we think is in and of itself a reflection of some of the characteristics of God. God has thoughts that exceed the mind that He blessed mankind with. He declares through Isaiah:

> "For My thoughts are not your thoughts,
> neither are your ways My ways,"
> declares the Lord.
> "As the heavens are higher than the earth,
> so are My ways higher than your ways
> and My thoughts than your thoughts." (Isaiah 55:8–9
> NIV)

God has a level of thinking that humanity cannot approach. As fallen creatures, we reject the mind of the Lord until regenerated by the Spirit of God. Regeneration allows us to possess the potential to think in a manner that glorifies and reflects the holiness of God. We can begin the process of fulfilling our potential for divine thinking by allowing our minds to be sanctified and redeemed by the Spirit of God through the Word of God.

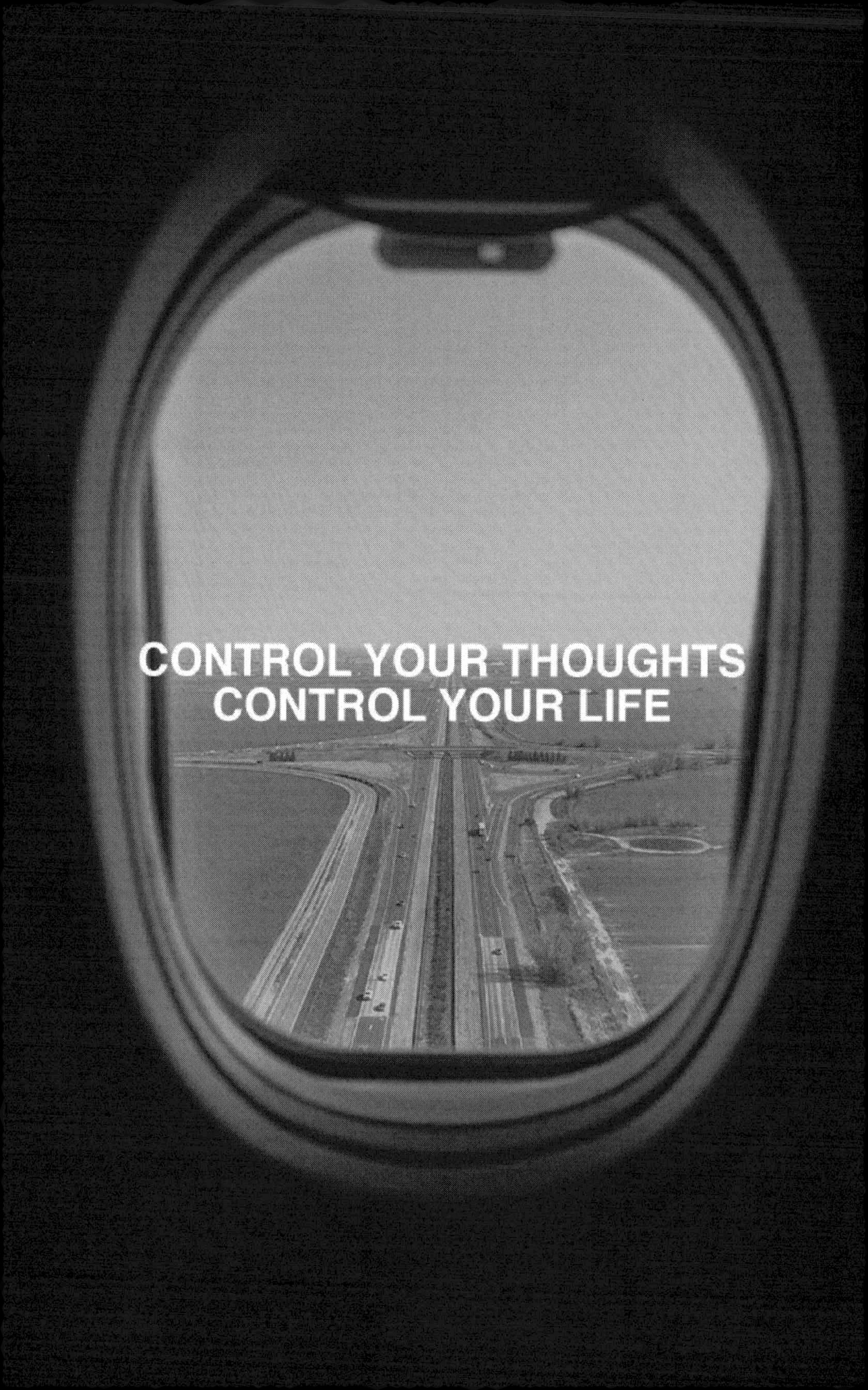
CONTROL YOUR THOUGHTS
CONTROL YOUR LIFE

Our minds have a tendency to dwell on depraved, debased things rather than on things that honor God. Due to the finished work of the cross, our inheritance is the mind of Christ. Yet, we often settle for a mind consumed by thoughts that direct our lives down paths that do not apprehend the high call of God.

Thoughts are the beginning of a process that leads to life or death. Thoughts lead to decision, decision leads to action, action leads to lifestyle, and lifestyle leads to destiny.

Control your thoughts, control your life.

Controlling thoughts is a battle, a fight. Depressive episodes have a way of beginning as a single thought. Many times, I can feel an episode coming when I wake up. Often, it starts as a single, small, seemingly insignificant thought in the morning. If allowed to live, if allowed to fester, that thought takes root and begins to grow and grow and grow and grow. What started as a minuscule thought blossoms into a full-on depressive episode, depriving my day of joy. If you have dealt with depression, you will know the phenomenon I am referring to. One negative, detrimental thought, allowed to survive, can trigger a litany of symptoms.

Growing up as a male pastor's kid, a frequent theme discussed in our home was purity. By purity, I am referring to saving sex for marriage and abstaining from activity that would jeopardize that. One day, after failing to "bounce my eyes" on multiple occasions, I sought out my pastor for counsel. What he said has stuck with me for decades. He explained that thoughts are like birds. His exact quote was, "Just because a bird lands in a tree doesn't mean you have to let it lay a nest."

Brilliant.

Now, let's get off of sex and back to invisible illness. Allow me to apply that idea to our thinking. Just because a negative, detrimental, worst-case-scenario thought pops into your head doesn't mean it must be allowed to remain and envelop all of your attention and focus. Shoo away that bird. Or, to put it Biblically, "Take captive every thought."

The Bible and Our Thoughts

Paul, in writing to the church in Corinth, explains what the life of a Christian should consist of and begins to delve into the fight we are to fight.

> For though we live in the world, we do not wage war as the world does. The weapons we fight with are not the weapons of the world. On the contrary, they have divine power to demolish strongholds. We demolish arguments and every pretension that sets itself up against the knowledge of God, and *we take captive every thought to make it obedient to Christ.* (2 Corinthians 10:3–5 NIV, emphasis mine)

In referring to a fight we are to fight, notice Paul highlights the importance of taking captive our thoughts. He uses the Greek word *aichmalotizo*, which literally refers to taking someone or something prisoner. Paul says we must take prisoner our thoughts that are not submitted to the Lordship of Jesus.

This begs the question: What thoughts are submitted to the Lordship of Jesus? I am so incredibly glad you asked. Paul has a handy answer for you in his letter to the Philippians:

> Finally, brothers and sisters, whatever is true, whatever is noble, whatever is right, whatever is pure, whatever is lovely, whatever is admirable—if anything is excellent or praiseworthy—think about such things. (Philippians 4:8 NIV)

Paul clearly dictates what things we are designed to meditate on—what things we are to ruminate on. Any thought that fails to measure up to this clear Biblical standard should be discarded as garbage. We must not allow useless thoughts to occupy the landscape of our minds. Take captive every thought. Don't allow a free-for-all in your mind. Your mind is not an MMA Octagon. It's not a bare-knuckle brawl. Take control. Let your thoughts reflect the nature and character of God. Meditate on things that produce the kind of fruit you want to see manifest in your life. Take a moment right now and meditate on these verses (all emphases mine):

> Since, then, you have been raised with Christ, set your hearts on things above, where Christ is, seated at the right hand of God. *Set your minds on things above, not on earthly things.* (Colossians 3:1–2 NIV)

Therefore, I urge you, brothers and sisters, in view of God's mercy, to offer your bodies as a living sacrifice, holy and pleasing to God—this is your true and proper worship. Do not conform to the pattern of this world, but *be transformed by the renewing of your mind.* Then you will be able to test and approve what God's will is—His good, pleasing and perfect will. (Romans 12:1–2 NIV)

For, "Who has known the mind of the Lord so as to instruct him?" But we have the mind of Christ. (1 Corinthians 2:16 NIV)

You will keep in perfect peace
all who trust in You,
all whose thoughts are fixed on You! (Isaiah 26:3)

This portion of Scripture in Isaiah is absolutely stunning. God promises to keep in perfect peace all whose thoughts are fixed on Jesus. The ESV reads, "whose mind is stayed on You." A stayed mind, with thoughts fixed on the beauty and supremacy of Jesus, yields a harvest of perfect peace. Let us fix our thoughts, take captive our thoughts, and direct them onto our King, Jesus.

Let us refuse to allow thoughts to meander through the recesses of our minds, clinging to dark corners and producing bouts of invisible illness. Take prisoner, take captive, forcefully navigate the focus of your mind onto the magnificence of your Savior.

Mind over Matter

In a previous chapter, we discussed in extremely vague, and general terms the makeup of our brains. Our brains are the control centers of our bodies. They can also be seen as intricate freeway systems, directing the traffic of feeling, emotion, thoughts, and other stimuli. As more studies have been conducted on the complexities of the human brain, the moldability of our brains continues to confound researchers. The human brain has what is called *neuroplasticity*. In laymen's terms, that means your brain is constantly being shaped and molded. Your brain is not like the femur—a bone that stays mostly the same throughout your life. The brain is constantly adapting to the stimuli that it processes.

Your thoughts actually create highways for communication in your brain. Thoughts create grooves and "trails". Signals, like water, find the path of least resistance. Therefore, they will travel through the grooves, or trails, that already exist.

If you have created a trail through negative, toxic thinking, a loop will be created using the path of least resistance. In turn, your gut reaction when faced with various seasons of life will be to view events through that negative lens. The highways we create through our thinking establish habits in our minds—habits toward positive, uplifting thinking or habits toward toxic thinking. Dr. Caroline Leaf says it this way:

> In the busyness of life and the flurry of everyday activity, we expose ourselves to the possibility of

developing a chaotic mindset with the net result of neurochemical and electromagnetic chaos in the brain. This feels like endless loops and spirals of thinking that can easily get out of control.[1]

In other words, science would recommend we "take captive our thoughts" for the good of our brain health. Dr. Leaf continues:

> The deeper you think, the more change you can make... If you don't get rid of the thought, you reinforce it.
> Don't forget, as a neuroplastician, you can do your own brain surgery. This means no thought should ever be allowed to control you.

J. P. Moreland states:

> Neuroplasticity refers to the brain's ability to form new brain grooves (i.e., new patterns of synaptic connections) and undergo a change of structure. The brain is not stuck in a static, unchanging structure. In fact, through repeated habit-forming practices of different ways of thinking, feeling, and behaving, one can reshape one's brain in a healthy direction.[2]

Negative thoughts create negative realities, both mentally and in your physical brain. We must control what thoughts we allow and discard toxic thinking. Karen Lawson, MD, wrote on the dangers of negative thinking for the University of Minnesota, and she had this to say:

> Negative attitudes and feelings of helplessness and hopelessness can create chronic stress, which upsets the body's hormone balance, depletes the brain chemicals required for happiness, and damages the immune system. Chronic stress can actually decrease our lifespan.[3]

Negative thinking produces negative results. The difficulty comes with the chicken or the egg question. Does mental illness cause negative thinking, or does negative thinking spur on mental illness? Like most answers in this book, I believe the answer is: both. Those of us who deal with invisible illness may have ingrained propensities toward negative thoughts. One writer suggested, "Whilst everyone experiences negative thoughts now and again, negative thinking that seriously affects the way you think about yourself and the world and even interferes with work/study and everyday functioning could be a symptom of a mental illness."[4]

Many of us who deal with invisible illness day in and day out may lean toward the negative, imagining worst-case scenarios over and over. Yet, we cannot allow negative thinking to become commonplace. If we let our guard down, we simply perpetuate the problem and limit our ability to heal. We are not victims; we are victors. Our propensities do not define us. We must not settle for the convenient; we must strive for what is healthy. Toxic thoughts impede our ability to negate the effects of mental illness. If you want to start a process of healing from invisible illness, one of the first steps is being intentional about what thoughts you allow to dominate your mind.

The good news is that, because our brains are moldable— because we possess neuroplasticity—new grooves and new highways can be formed. In the same way that negative thinking can become habitual, based on the pattern of our responses and thoughts, positive, glass-half-full thinking can create new habits and grooves in our brains. We have the ability to rewire our brains to view the world in a positive light. The question is, How do we do this? Let's talk about some practicalities.

1. Read the Word of God

Scripture is the best way to begin to rewire our brains. Paul writes to the Roman church in Romans 12 to "be transformed by the renewing of your mind." When we allow God to speak to us through His Word—when we submit the whole of our lives, including our thought life, to the infallibility of Scripture— our minds can be renewed. Our thoughts purified. We gain a renewed focus.

Paul writes to the church in Ephesus in chapter 5 of Ephesians, addressing marriage and how husbands and wives are to interact with each other and prefer each other. Marriage reflects the relationship Jesus has with His Church; His bride. He tells husbands they are to treat their wives as Jesus treats

His Bride. One of Paul's examples directly applies to what we are discussing here:

> Husbands, love your wives, just as Christ loved the church and gave Himself up for her to make her holy, cleansing her by the washing with water through the Word. (Ephesians 5:25–26 NIV)

There is a cleansing that takes place as we delve into Scripture. If you are having problems with your thought life, start by diving into Scripture. Learn how to study your Bible in context, with a historical understanding in concert with the saints and patriarchs of old. Allow orthodoxy and overall historic agreement to influence your understanding of the text. Memorize, recite, and meditate on Scripture daily. Much of Scripture is known as ancient meditation literature, meaning that the best way to understand and glean fruitful results is *not* to skim through your Bible-reading plan or pluck Scripture out of context to help motivate you for a football game. The most fruitful way to study Scripture is by reading and rereading and meditating on its meaning over a period of days and years and a lifetime.

2. Confession

Our words have power. Life and death are in the power of the tongue. Toxic thoughts are like the Hulk. The Hulk is already beastly strong, but he gets stronger the madder he gets. Your thoughts already have power, but when you verbalize toxic thoughts, you multiply their efficacy.

Let's walk through an example. Let's say the negative thought you have is, *I'm fat and worthless.* That thought is no good, not a winner. If you allow that thought to run a marathon in your mind, and you pump it with some steroids by verbalizing, "I'm fat and worthless", not only did you think a negative thought, but then you heard yourself saying, "I'm fat and worthless", thus reinforcing toxic thinking.

Confession is powerful.

In the book of James, the author is writing to what is referred to as the *diaspora*, which is the twelve tribes of Israel scattered abroad. In chapter 5, he addresses the power of prayer and the detrimental effects of sin, and then he states a spiritual reality many of us miss:

> Therefore confess your sins to each other and pray for each other so that you may be healed. The prayer of a righteous person is powerful and effective. (James 5:16 NIV)

Obviously, the context here is confessing sin to other believers, but I want to simply draw your attention to the weight God places on confession. Don't miss the Biblical truth here: healing comes from confessing sins one to another. Forgiveness comes through confessing our sins to God, who is "faithful and just to forgive us." But in His sovereignty, God has allowed healing to come also through person-to-person confession. So many Christ followers are walking around forgiven but not healed—

forgiven by God yet walking in brokenness, because their confession to one another is lacking.

When we confess the truth of what God has said, we reap the benefits.

Confess the Scriptures.
Confess the promises of God.
Confess who God said you are.
Refuse to settle for confessing the lies of the enemy.

Throughout Scripture, you see examples of individuals declaring the goodness of God, confessing who He is, and lifting their voices to proclaim the truth of God. I'm not referring to some new-age, name-it-and-claim-it, *The Secret*–type voodoo stuff. I'm speaking to the tried-and-true Scripture pattern of reminding yourself vocally about who God is and allowing yourself to hear yourself. Here is one quick example. After this, I encourage you to dive into the book of Psalms, and you will see the pattern repeatedly.

> I will lift my voice to sing Your praise, O my
> Strength—
> for You came to my defense.
> O God, You have shown me Your loving mercy.
> (Psalm 59:17 VOICE)

3. Take captive every thought

Let's end this chapter with this easier-said-than-done step. To get our thought life on track, we have to do the hard work of "bouncing" toxic thinking. We can't allow ourselves to ruminate on non-life-giving thinking. We do not have the margin or mental bandwidth to manage the negative effects of toxic thinking.

At the end of the day, to change the manner in which we think, self-discipline will need to be employed. But here is the beautiful thing: one of the by-products of being full of the Spirit of God is self-control. The more time we spend with God—the more time we spend in worship, in prayer, and in the Word— the more we leak the fruit of the Spirit. If you are lacking self-control, spend some more one-on-one time with God. I can't emphasize enough how vital our alone time with God is. We are unable to live a successful, overcoming life as Christ followers without a vibrant devotional life. If we want to leak love, joy, peace, patience, kindness, goodness, faithfulness, gentleness, and self-control—all the fruit of the Spirit—we have to be full of the Spirit. You are full of whatever you consume the most (we will discuss this in depth in a later chapter).

Taking captive our thoughts means employing self-control and not permitting ourselves to entertain any thoughts that do not line up with the truth of Scripture. Jesus said not to worry, so we refuse to worry. Jesus said we are His friends, so we force our confession to line up with that truth. Scripture says we are beautifully and wonderfully made, knit together in our mother's wombs, so we reject any thinking to the contrary. *Take captive* every thought. *Take* is an active word, not a passive word. To rewire our thinking for the benefit of our mental health, we must be proactive and focus our thoughts on truth.

Having a healthy thought life is vital in our pursuit of healing. If we are going to find any measure of healing from our invisible illness, we need to reject toxic thinking and cling to life-giving thinking. Remember, we are what we think. So, think good thoughts—healthy, life-giving, epic thoughts.

CHAPTER 8

SCOREBOARDS

> *We won't be distracted by comparison if we are captivated with purpose.*
>
> *—Bob Goff*

I remember the exact moment I saw my wife for the first time. She was like a prancing gazelle in the Sahara and—me—I was the prowling lion. Hungry for a honey. Drooling, admiring God's handiwork and the way He molded this fine young lass. I was an idiotic high-school sophomore whose confession that I simply wanted to "encounter God" at a youth conference was an unconvincing cover for, "I'm trying to meet some ladies."

As a sophomore, I thought I had *drip*, *swag*, or insert here whatever the kids are saying these days for "thought I was good with women." The stark reality is that **NO** fifteen-year-old has game. I was no exception. Wielding my best pick-up line, I began to approach my prey, my confidence sky-high. The results could not have been further from expectation. My wife shut me down in a hot second. She don't play.

Years later, I found her again. The year was 2005, and a world-changing playground, pregnant with the ability to rekindle long-lost love, was bursting onto the scene: Myspace. As the youth say, I slid into her DMs, and after what I would call persistence (some might say stalking), the rest is history.

Myspace was a gamechanger. In an instant, an expansive, seemingly ever-expanding world shrank down into 140 characters or less. Losing touch after high school or college is now a thing of bygone eras. We've never been more connected. At the touch of a button, thousands of profiles, faces, and relationships are available to explore. Now there are thousands of social-media platforms, all clamoring for our attention and crying out, "You NEED me!" While researching this topic, one article title stood out to me. It is titled "75+ Social Media Sites You Need to Know in 2020."[1] Think about that statement: 75+ social media sites we need to know.

This article claims, "While there weren't even a billion people using social media back in 2010, the number exceeded more than 2 billion within just five years. In 2019, around 2.77 billion people were using social media." Based on those stats, a third of the people on the planet are engaged in social media. Think about it—how many people do you personally know who are 100 percent off social media? Anyone? If you know someone, they are the oddball, the abnormality, the weirdo. Social media is what *we do* now.

In fact, the Pew Research center reports that 81 percent of American teens and 69 percent of American adults frequent social media.[2] One survey reported 57 percent of its respondents check social media every day, yet the American Psychological Association reports 86 percent of individuals would fall into the category lovingly referred to as a "constant checker."[3]

Social media is a constant in our lives partly because of its addictive nature. It has been purposely engineered to engage with the reward centers in our brains. The likes and comments are intentionally designed to release dopamine (known as the "feel-good" chemical). Dopamine is released by sex, good food, social interaction, and now, thanks to brilliant engineers, social media. The apps are designed to unveil new content with every swipe. It's like a slot machine—every time you refresh, there just might be something new. There could be some much-needed affirmation.

Could there be new likes?
Could there be new followers?
Could there be newly tagged photos?

All of these things are intentionally engineered to get you to spend your time on their platforms. Edward Tufte said it this way: "There are only two industries that call their customers 'users': illegal drugs and software."[4] One study showed that social media may even be more addictive than cigarettes and alcohol.[5]

John Mark Comer brilliantly says: "The problem is, even if we realize and admit that we have a digital addiction—it's an *addiction*. Our willpower doesn't stand a chance against the Like button."[6]

Due to the widespread nature of social-media use, it would be prudent to find out what effects social media may have on our mental health. Does social media use have solely noble purposes and effects, or are there some underlying, hidden, dangerous consequences lurking around the bend? To science we go!

Comparison Trap

If you are above the age of twenty-five, you remember what it was like not to know what was happening everywhere all the time. My brother and I use to fight over phone use vs. Internet use. Remember when you had to choose between talking to your long-lost love on the phone or surfing AOL?

One at a time—either plug in the phone, or plug in the computer.
Choices, choices.

We used to have the ability to live in naivety. Not knowing what tragedies are transpiring around the globe is a luxury of the past. The famous adage rings true: ignorance truly was bliss.

Recently, I asked my mom what she would have had to do to find out what was happening in China when she was a kid. She sighed, clearly remembering inconvenient memories. "I would have had to go to the library and tear through newspapers, periodicals, and magazines. It would take hours, and it might have still been dated." Today, I ask Siri, and my wish is her command.

As an infamous millennial, I am a part of the last generation to remember what life was like pre-Internet, pre-DSL, pre-smartphone. When the iPhone came out when I was a senior in high school, it seemed too good to be true. Directions without MapQuest? Witchcraft!

In 1998, a few scholars met in an effort to compile the effects of Internet use in the home. They concluded children who spent time online regularly exhibited a decrease in social interaction with both friends and family, and there was a spike in negative emotions, such as loneliness, isolation, and depression.[7] Keep in mind, this study was conducted in 1998. Social media didn't exist. These findings were the conclusion of research conducted on dial-up Internet.

Now, with the explosion of social media, face-to-face time seems to be on a steep decline, and the effects of extended social media use do not seem to be positive. My goal is not to slam the use of social media. I believe social media is a tool.

Like all tools, social media can be used for noble, amazing purposes. However, like most things, when not used in moderation, it can be destructive.

Social media has become a scoreboard, allowing individuals to know if they are winning or losing at life. The problem is, the opponent we face is a concoction of airbrush and highlight reels. We are comparing our real selves to fake, imaginary caricatures. Let's look at two scoreboards.

Scoreboard #1: Appearance

With the advent of filters within social media platforms, users can edit themselves to look exactly how they wish they looked in real life. Celebrities used to be the only ones with the advantage of airbrush. Now, twelve-year-old hormonal adolescent children, whose insecurity is already at an all-time high due to their changing bodies, have the ability to edit themselves on demand. This ability to filter away insecurity is manifesting itself in a boom in the plastic-surgery arena. Tijion Esho, a cosmetic doctor, coined the term "Snapchat dysmorphia" to describe the phenomenon of patients desiring to look like their filtered selfies. Esho says social media can create "unrealistic expectations of what is normal."[8]

In the past, patients would bring in the spreads of their favorite celebrities, expressing their desire to look like "that". Now they bring in photos of themselves doctored up by their social-media app of choice, desiring to look like a fake version of themselves. Natural is not good enough when everyone else on the virtual scoreboard embodies perfection.

In 2017, the American Academy of Facial Plastic and Reconstructive Surgery reported that 55 percent of its surgeons cited "looking better in selfies" as being the cause for their patients going under the knife. That number is 13 percent higher than the previous year. Experts are finding that Snapchat dysmorphia can actually lead to body dysmorphic disorder (BDD), a disorder in the family of obsessive-compulsive disorder.[9] This disorder manifests itself in several ways, including constant mirror checking and obsessive comparison. Research has shown that individuals who are inflicted with BDD may "experience lifetime suicidal ideation, and 24% to 28% have attempted suicide."[10] One article published in *JAMA Facial Plastic Surgery* by scholars from Boston University School of Medicine's Department of Dermatology concludes that social media altering the way we view ourselves "is an alarming trend because those filtered selfies often present an unattainable look and are blurring the line of reality and fantasy for these patients."[11]

Comparing our real lives to fantasy is the norm in today's society, and, by the way, this is horrific for our mental health.

Imagine for a moment if I worked out religiously, pumping iron with vigor. Imagine if my goal was to don the physique of the Incredible Hulk. I wore the purple shorts, refused to wear a shirt or shoes, and claimed I would, one day, look like the green Avenger himself. Now follow me here—what if every time I looked in the mirror, I was angry and disillusioned because I did not look like the angry, green superhero? The vast majority of rational humans would think my emotions were completely irrational. Why? Because I am comparing my real human body to fiction. I am comparing myself to a fake person.

As ludicrous as that example may sound, many of us fall victim to this very scenario, as our thumbs double-tap and swipe up and down. Comparison sweeps in as we view the lives of those we know and love, living their best lives while we live our average lives. We compare our human, natural selves to processed, photoshopped, fake bodies and wonder why depression seeps in. As we view, we are checking the proverbial scoreboard and coming to the conclusion we are losing.

Scoreboard #2: Social Life

We compare our bodies, and we also compare our lives as a whole. We end up comparing the reality of our lives with carefully curated and cultivated profiles of people's preferred realities. We typically only post the perfect angles, the perfect food, and the perfect moments and tend to neglect moments of weakness and the angles that show the fifteen-pound weight gain. Our sense of self is coming from how we think we are doing in life compared to others.

I am "x" because I have done "y."
I am "x" because I am doing better than him/her.
Comparison is a trap.

One article phrases it this way: "The self can now be packaged as a product."[12] Who we are on social media does not have to be who we really are. What we see on social media does not have to be tethered to reality. And often, it's not.

It's fiction.
It's counterfeit.

Who we are is often based on comparing ourselves to other people. Yet, we weren't designed to find our identity in comparison. As we live our normal, daily lives, complete with our nine-to-five, our digital scoreboards are faithful to remind us of so-and-so's trip to Bali, their new promotion, their perfect spouse. We are left comparing our real, messy lives to a concocted highlight reel and concluding we are failures because of the discrepancy.

I remember days of going to school thinking all was well in the world. The grass was green, and the sky was blue, complete with *Toy Story* clouds and a slight breeze. Everything was fine, until I found out about little Billy's party last night that *everyone* was at. That is, everyone but me. I wasn't invited. I was totally fine until *that* moment, because I was informed of what I had missed out on.

I think we all have stories of realizing we missed out on something. The problem is that now we are constantly being reminded of what we are missing. Missing out on the perfect job, the perfect spouse and kids, the social event—we missed it.

We failed.

And we are afraid to do so again.

FOMO is the term—*fear of missing out*.

Our world is leading us into a comparison trap that is sucking the life out of our souls. Social media is a scoreboard, and we are buying into the lie that we are losing.

Social Media and Mental Health

Now that we have fifteen-plus years of data on social media, we are seeing the repercussions of a social-media-infused society. The vast majority of youth and young adults are on social media (see chart[13]).

Social Media Platform	Percentage of 13–17-year-olds using	Percentage of 18–24-year-olds using
Snapchat	69	78
Instagram	72	71
Facebook	51	80
Twitter	32	45
YouTube	85	94

Large numbers of young people are reporting various experiences with mental illness. One study says, "The rate of individuals reporting symptoms consistent with major depression in the last 12 months increased 52 percent in adolescents from 2005 to 2017 (from 8.7 percent to 13.2 percent), and 63 percent in young adults age 18 to 25 from 2009 to 2017 (from 8.1 percent to 13.2 percent)."[14]

Now, I know correlation doesn't always equate to causality, but I'm going to play the devil's advocate for a moment. Comb over the statistics from that last quote for a moment and follow me here. Myspace sold for $580 million in 2006, meaning its meteoric rise was imminent in 2005. The year 2009 marked the dawning of the smartphone age. The year 2007 saw the first iPhone released. Could it be that our dependence on and overindulgence in social media and technology are playing into the rise in symptoms of mental illness? Many, many psychologists, sociologists, and doctors believe so.

One study found an alarming statistical relationship between high school students' time spent on social media and depressive symptoms. The greater the time on social media, the greater the depressive symptoms.[15]

Another study argues that the evidence points to greater social-media use being associated with "higher depressive and anxiety scores, poor sleep, low self-esteem, and body-image concerns."[16]

Other reports show a link between young-adult users nineteen to thirty-two interacting with multiple social-media platforms and an increase in symptoms related to anxiety and depression.[17]

The numbers are coming out, and it seems pretty clear that the virtual scoreboards called social media, when used in excess, are not good for our mental well-being. Many of us are allowing our identities to be shaped by virtual scoreboards. We were not designed to be defined and constrained by comparison.

Let me reiterate—comparison is a trap.
A snare.

Who We Are

If we aren't careful, we will allow the fantasy presented before us, rather than our Creator, to mold us. This has the power to destroy our mental well-being.

In the beginning, God saw potential in the dirt before Him. The Creator of the universe formed and molded humanity. He spent His time making humanity in His image and likeness. Then, He breathed the breath of life into our ancestors' nostrils. As the Author of creativity, He knows best how we function and are designed.

Adam and Eve turned their backs on the Creator and ran after their own selfish desires. Humanity has taken a play out of Adam and Eve's book ever since. We run toward our own desires, and in so doing, have lost what truly gave us value: a relationship with the Almighty. We are created in His image and likeness to share in dominion—to share in the family business. Yet, even in the midst of our sin, there is hope and the potential to regain the identity we were created to cling to.

Let me take a moment and remind us who we are when we are in Christ.

> For those who are led by the Spirit of God are the children of God. The Spirit you received does not make you slaves, so that you live in fear again; rather, the Spirit you received brought about your adoption to sonship. And by Him we cry, "*Abba, Father*." The Spirit Himself testifies with our spirit that we are God's children. Now if we are children, then we are heirs—heirs of God and co-heirs with Christ, if indeed we share in His sufferings in order that we may also share in His glory. (Romans 8:14–17 NIV)

Scripture is clear that by submitting the whole of our lives to the Lordship of Christ, by turning from our sin, by believing God raised Jesus from the dead, and by believing that Jesus is the Son of God, salvation comes to us. Salvation is not a result of works. Salvation is not a matter of earning or striving. Salvation is the result of the profound, extravagant grace of God. Paul explains that the deposit of the Spirit of God within us began a good work, culminating in our sonship. We no longer identify with our brokenness and sin; we stand in Christ, taking on sonship while being stripped of slavery. The Almighty God now sees us through the lens of all that Jesus accomplished on the cross. His blood cries out, "Forgiven, penalty paid." Sonship is our portion when Christ is our Lord. That is who we are.

In light of that, comparison is ridiculous. Who am I to devalue what Christ deemed worthy of His sacrifice? Why would I compare my life to another creation? I am to live in gratitude, reflecting on His grace and marveling at His goodness. We have the propensity to take things with divine potential and turn them into tools of destruction for our minds. We must not allow what we see to determine who we are. Our identity is in Christ alone.

Training Wheels

So, what do we do now? Do we reject all technology and delete every social-media platform? No, I don't believe that is the answer. Every tool can be abused, but when used correctly, we can reap the rewards. Here are some super-practical and some spiritual steps I would suggest:

1. Allow Christ to define your identity

First and foremost, we must be found in Christ. Who we are is not based on our strength and sufficiency, but we must allow the truth of Scripture to define us. I stand on the finished work of the cross and allow that to define me. My failures and shortcomings pass through the filter of the cross. My insecurity passes through the filter of the cross. I am who Christ says I am, as defined in Scripture. Know the Word, and allow that to define you.

Social media is a great tool, but whether I have two followers or 200,000 followers, my identity is unchanged. I am in Christ. No one can change that.

PSALM 9:1 NIV

"I WILL GIVE THANKS
TO YOU LORD, WITH
ALL MY HEART; I WILL
TELL OF ALL YOUR
WONDERFUL DEEDS."

2. Reduce time online

It is easier not to feel like you are losing if you don't look at the digital scoreboard. Many of us need a brain detox. Get off online platforms as much as possible. The University of Pennsylvania conducted research that found that "reducing social media use to 30 minutes a day resulted in a significant reduction in levels of anxiety, depression, loneliness, sleep problems, and FOMO."[18]

I would recommend setting app time limits on your phone, disabling all notifications, and limiting how often you check your phone.

3. Live thankfully

An easy way to avoid scoreboards is to realize you really *are* winning in life. Recall what God has already done. Recall His faithfulness. Take some time right now to meditate on and declare the following verses. Take a little praise break.

> I will give thanks to You, LORD, with all my heart;
> I will tell of all Your wonderful deeds. (Psalm 9:1)

> Enter His gates with thanksgiving
> and His courts with praise;
> give thanks to Him and praise His name.
> For the LORD is good and His love endures forever;
> His faithfulness continues through all generations.
> (Psalm 100:4–5)

> Be filled with the Spirit, speaking to one another with psalms, hymns, and songs from the Spirit. Sing and make music from your heart to the Lord, always giving thanks to God the Father for everything, in the name of our Lord Jesus Christ. (Ephesians 5:18–20)

> Do not be anxious about anything, but in every situation, by prayer and petition, with thanksgiving, present your requests to God. And the peace of God, which transcends all understanding, will guard your hearts and your minds in Christ Jesus. (Philippians 4:6–7)

> So then, just as you received Christ Jesus as Lord, continue to live your lives in Him, rooted and built up in Him, strengthened in the faith as you were taught, and overflowing with thankfulness. (Colossians 2:6–7)

No matter what life is throwing at you, you have a lot to be thankful for. Wake up each morning and recall some things you are thankful for. It's amazing what will happen if we simply live thankfully.

4. Spend more time with friends offline than online

We cannot allow virtual relationships to replace our real, flesh-and-blood relationships. I hate to be the bearer of bad news, but your Facebook friends aren't your real friends. Your

Instagram followers aren't your real pals. We need real people in our lives and in our corner. Invest your time in real relationships rather than simply spending time in virtual spaces. I would encourage you to dedicate time every week investing in friends and family. Laugh, have fun, and enjoy life. We all need people, real people. As the adage goes, laughter is the best medicine. I believe laughter is best with friends.

Social media is a great tool that can be abused and misused or redeemed to reap great rewards. When it's misused, we find ourselves hurting and disillusioned; when it's redeemed, we find ourselves well connected.

Let's not allow a tool to become an entity that ensnares our mental faculties and devolves our sense of self to comparison. You matter; people matter. God is good. Let's be thankful and stand firm in Christ.

CHAPTER 9

SABBATH

> *Rest and motion, unrelieved and unchecked, are equally destructive.*
>
> —Benjamin Cardozo

Sabbath: a concept that seems antiquated. Rest is for the weak; rest is for the sluggard, the lazy. I'll rest when I'm dead. The culture we are entrenched in scoffs at the idea of a Sabbath—a weekly time simply for rest and worship. Wayne Muller says it this way:

> While many of us are terribly weary, we have come to associate tremendous guilt and shame with taking time to rest.[1]

Speed and hurry are seen as necessary to survive in our culture. Society is continuing a progression toward faster paces and less rest as technology advances, and our lust for more increases. We can know more than ever before; we can do and are doing more than ever before. Psychologists are seeing a trend in what they are calling "hurry sickness," which can be defined as "a behavior pattern characterized by continual rushing and anxiousness; an overwhelming and continual sense of urgency."[2] Ask ten people how they are doing, and I guarantee the overwhelming responses will either be "tired" or "busy." We are busy, we run, we work, and we overwork. The irony is that studies show we actually become less productive when we overwork.[3] Currently, it is estimated that 51 percent of Americans haven't gone a vacation in a year, and 36 percent have not vacationed in two years.[4] One study surveyed eleven thousand adults and concluded that there were 653.9 million wasted vacation days in 2018.[5] In 2004, National Health Interview Survey concluded that 30 percent of adults sleep less than six hours per night.[6] We work more, live at breakneck speeds, restless, vacation less, and wonder why our minds are unable to find peace.

John Mark Comer says, "Hurry is a form of violence on the soul."[7]

We were not designed to function in a constant state of rush and busyness. We must rest.

The Order of Things

"In the beginning, God created the heavens and the earth."
We know this as the opening of Scripture, Genesis 1:1. The
earth was formless until the Creator began His work of creating.
The Potter used the vast expanse of the universe as clay, as He
sculpted what would be the humble beginnings of human
history. He spoke, authoring life. He breathed the stars;
Scripture declares He knows them by name. He created
vegetation, lifecycles, night and day, the sun and moon. For six
days, He toiled and worked, enjoying the fruits of His labor.
And then God rested.

God, the Author of everything, *THE* Beginning and End, rested.
He took an entire day to look at His work and simply rest.

This is the beginning of the Sabbath. The word "Sabbath" is
taken from the Jewish word *shavat,* which simply means "*to
rest.*" Throughout Scripture, you see the Israelites following the
example of their God and resting on the Sabbath. In fact, God
commands rest.

> Remember the Sabbath day by keeping it holy. Six
> days you shall labor and do all your work, but the
> seventh day is a Sabbath to the Lord your God. On
> it you shall not do any work, neither you, nor your
> son or daughter, nor your male or female servant,
> nor your animals, nor any foreigner residing in your
> towns. For in six days the Lord made the heavens
> and the earth, the sea, and all that is in them, but he

rested on the seventh day. Therefore the Lord blessed the Sabbath day and made it holy. (Exodus 20:8–11 NIV)

Notice the word *remember*. The Hebrew word used for *remember* means … "to remember." God knows the tendency of the human condition is forgetfulness. We move on, rush past, continue on to something new and flashy. Yet, with the Sabbath, God commands that we remember, and we do so by keeping it holy. To keep something holy means to value something, to set it apart from other things, not to treat it as common. The Sabbath, from the beginning, has been a day to value and esteem—to treat as uncommon and to remember.

God commands that we work six days and rest on the seventh. We model His week and set our lives up to match His rhythm. Built into the fabric of the Sabbath is faith. Faith is believing that God is who He says He is and will do what He says He will do. In Greek, "faith" is *pistis,* which simply means "*confidence.*" Faith is confidence in God.

Now faith is the substance of things hoped for, the evidence of things not seen. (Hebrews 11:1 NKJV)

By observing the Sabbath, your body language expresses confidence in God to provide. We take Him at His Word and rest, believing He will take care of all things. A lack of rest speaks of striving, of self-reliance. Self-reliance has no place in the walk of faith. The walk of faith is a walk of stewarding what we have been trusted with, while obeying God in everything.

Wayne Muller says, "The Sabbath teaching was clear: Nothing really belongs to us. It is all—lands, wealth, loved ones, life itself—on loan from God."[8]

From the beginning, God set the example of how the rhythm of our lives should be.
Hustle six days, rest one.
Hustle six days, rest one.

God took the Sabbath so seriously that He even commanded a Sabbath for the land.

> But in the seventh year there shall be a Sabbath of solemn rest for the land, a Sabbath to the Lord. You shall neither sow your field nor prune your vineyard. (Leviticus 25:4 NKJV)

In observing the Sabbath rest for the land, God promises that the land will produce more in six years with His blessing than seven years with solely human effort. God is serious about rest and Sabbath.

However, as humans do, we have twisted the Sabbath to mean and be something it was never intended to be. The priests and scribes wrote guidelines around the law of the Sabbath to ensure that no one got close to encroaching upon it. It became an infringement on the law to carry the tool of your trade on the Sabbath. Rather than simply being a day of rest and worship, the Sabbath became an obligatory mandate with severe punishment if one neglected to observe it.

A Gift to Be Opened

My birthday is on Christmas Day. Yes, Christmas Day. Clearly, hours of labor and birthing a nine-pound, ten-ounce baby was the best gift my mom ever received for Christmas. As you can imagine, having a birthday on Christmas complicates things. When I was a kid, I could never have a birthday party on my birthday or rarely even in the month of December, due to all of my friends either being on vacation or at compulsory family get-togethers. I could deal with this; July parties are better anyway—why would I settle for a December party when I could opt for a slip n' slide?

By far, the worst part about a Christmas birthday is the gift-giving debacle. You find out who your cheap friends are pretty quickly. Too many to count settled for the "this-is-for-your-birthday-AND-Christmas" cover-up.

"Thanks for $5.12 to Subway, Brandon. You shouldn't have…"

My parents, however, did the best they could to make the day special. Christmas morning would come, and all four kids would converge on the tree, igniting what resembled a Santa-themed gift-wrap tornado, flailing and flinging paper, bags, and boxes about, seeking for treasure just on the other end of mystery. My parents would sit back, camcorder in hand, my dad in his signature maroon-and-grey plaid robe, enjoying the glee their generosity provided.

After the morning festivities and a day filled with coffee, food, and the NBA, dinner came. Dinner was all about my birthday.

Year after year, they did their best to ensure my birthday dinner was special, unique. The dinner was capped off by the entrance of a cake with candles lit and my family bellowing, "Happy Birthday", my dad hitting the high harmonies with ease.

And then, my birthday presents.
My parents would wrap my birthday gifts in birthday wrapping paper, not Christmas paper. They were special gifts—they made sure of it. Massive grins were painted across their faces, as they handed me gifts they knew I would enjoy.

God has given us a gift; many of us ignore it and allow it to remain wrapped. That gift is the Sabbath. The Sabbath is a gift designed by God for His kids. Many of us stiff-arm the notion of the Sabbath, thinking we can endure a lack of rest.

It's not commendable.
It's not responsible.
It's not respectful toward a generous Father.

Jesus and the Sabbath

In the Gospel of Mark, Jesus is shown as the Servant Messiah, the Godman who came to serve and not be served, determined to save through substitutionary sacrifice. The opening of the Gospel highlights the herald of the Savior, John the Baptist, the voice crying out in the wilderness, followed by the temptation of Jesus, resulting in a victorious, Spirit-filled Savior stepping out into His earthly ministry. Jesus begins with miraculous signs and wonders accompanying His proclamation of the Kingdom of God invading human history. Demons are cast out; the sick are made well; a paralyzed man lowered through a hole bored through the roof is pulled to his feet. The miracles become commonplace as the LORD of lords walks the streets.

One Sabbath day, Jesus and His disciples are making their way through some grain fields. I imagine the fields ripe for harvest, the gold, slender stalks waving in the light breeze. The disciples pluck the grain, enjoying a light snack on their tour across the countryside. The religious leaders of the day are incensed by such a reckless and careless encroachment upon their Sabbath laws. Their laws forbade harvesting on the Sabbath, and, clearly, picking single heads of grain was akin to harvesting grain for the sake of profit. Jesus addresses the offense by harkening back to King David, a man on the Mount Rushmore of Jewish heroes, who broke the law concerning eating food in the House of God. Then He makes a statement that is beautiful and enlightening:

> Then He said to them, "The Sabbath was made for man, not man for the Sabbath." (Mark 2:27 NIV)

Jesus brings back the original intent of the Sabbath. The Sabbath was made for man, not man for the Sabbath. Sabbath is a gift from God to humanity, a gift that the Creator Himself partook of and then presented to humanity—a gift many of us have allowed to sit unopened, bow and all.

Rest is a beautiful gift from God, yet we reject it and cling to our own rhythms and cycles of life, not understanding that we are bucking the divine cycle of work and rest. When we reject the Sabbath, we reject the divine order of things.

As you read through the Gospels, notice how often Jesus withdraws to rest and worship:

> It was at this time that He went off to the mountain to pray, and He spent the whole night in prayer to God. (Luke 6:12)

> In the early morning, while it was still dark, Jesus got up, left the house, and went away to a secluded place, and was praying there. (Mark 1:35)

> But Jesus Himself would often slip away to the wilderness and pray. (Luke 5:16)

> The apostles gathered around Jesus and reported to Him all they had done and taught. Then, because so many people were coming and going that they did not even have a chance to eat, He said to them, "Come with Me by yourselves to a quiet place and get some rest." So they went away by themselves in a boat to a solitary place. (Mark 6:30–32 niv)

Jesus maintained a regular rhythm of hard work, followed by rest and worship. As followers of Christ, we would do well to mimic the life rhythm of our Savior. When we stiff-arm the gift of rest and neglect the divine rhythm we are to employ, we reap the results we see in today's culture.

Rest or Be Forced To

As discussed earlier, busy sickness is a real phenomenon that is infecting many of us who refuse to slow down. Leading hurried lives can result in stress, which we discussed in an earlier chapter, and its negative impacts on mental health. We can also be left feeling:

- Anxious
- Overwhelmed
- Inadequate
- Sad
- Frustrated
- Angry
- Lonely
- Hopeless
- Incompetent
- Guilty[9]

Our physical bodies can suffer:

- Muscle tension/pain
- Restlessness
- Insomnia
- Headaches
- Inflammation
- Compromised immune system
- Fatigue
- Change in sex drive
- Digestion issues

- Cardiovascular disease[10]

We are social beings, often gauging success by comparing ourselves to others. This ideology is called "social comparison theory", and it can be defined as "determining our own social and personal self-worth based on how we stack up against others we perceive as somehow faring better or worse."[11] The problem is, if we deem ourselves "behind", we often fill up our plates in an attempt to "catch up." Keeping up with the Joneses is impossible, but we scratch and claw in a rat race of who's got the most toys and the biggest house, and it is killing us. Jodi Clarke says, "When we glorify busyness, we are likely to overextend ourselves with varied obligations, appointments, commitments, and responsibilities."[11] In our culture, staying busy is a badge of honor.

We commend it.
Honor it.
Celebrate it.

But should we? Living lives that are always on the go can lead to mental exhaustion. Side effects of mental exhaustion can be low emotional resilience, feeling stressed or anxious, feelings of helplessness, chronic feelings of being overwhelmed, low motivation, depression, and suicidal thoughts.[12]

Wayne Muller says in his book *Sabbath*:

> A successful life has become a violent enterprise. We make war on our bodies, pushing them beyond their limits; war on our children, because we cannot

find enough time to be with them when they are hurt and afraid and need our company; war on our spirit, because we are too preoccupied to listen to the quiet voices that seek to nourish and refresh us; war on our communities, because we are fearfully protecting what we have and do not feel safe enough to be kind and generous; war on the earth, because we cannot take the time to place our feet on the ground and allow it to feed us, to taste its blessings and give thanks.[13]

Being successful, as many would define it in today's day and age, is harming our souls and our mental well-being.

Often, with our actions, we have decided that things and money are more valuable than time and relationships. Now, we may not say that with our mouths, but our lifestyles indicate where our priorities lie. Again from Wayne Muller:

We have traded our time for money... When presented with a choice between time and money, it is best to trade up, to trade lesser-valued time for greater-valued money. It is seen as the prudent, superior, and necessary act.[1]

Things cost more than they cost. Lifestyles cost more than the price tag. Price equates to earning, earning equates to time, time equates to life. So, in a roundabout way, our lifestyles equate to sacrificed time. Everything we buy costs time. Everything we do costs valuable time. I fear one of the greatest mistakes in the twenty-first century is valuing any temporal commodity above time. We cannot create more time with family—with loved ones we hold dear and cherish.

Beginning the Sabbath Process

My wife would be quick to tell you I am no expert on the practice of Sabbath. I find fulfillment in accomplishment—in the doing. I tend toward workaholism. I love my job; I could write, speak, and counsel all day every day. In fact, taking a break, taking time off, is a discipline for me. Years ago, when my mental health was at an all-time low, I was taking eighteen units in college, working three jobs, volunteering as a youth pastor, and trying to learn how to be married. I had no days off, and my mental health indicated that. I was forced to take time off because of a mental collapse. What I have found and seen over the years in my own life and in the lives of those I pastor is this: You will rest, or your body will force you to.

"WE DO NOT FEEL HOW MUCH ENERGY WE SPEND ON EACH ACTIVITY, BECAUSE WE IMAGINE WE WILL ALWAYS HAVE MORE ENERGY AT OUR DISPOSAL. THIS ONE LITTLE CONVERSATION, THIS ONE EXTRA PHONE CALL, THIS ONE QUICK MEETING, WHAT CAN IT COST? BUT IT DOES COST, IT DRAINS YET ANOTHER DROP OF OUR LIFE. THEN, AT THE END OF DAYS, WEEKS, MONTHS, YEARS, WE COLLAPSE, WE BURN OUT, AND CANNOT SEE WHERE IT HAPPENED. IT HAPPENED IN A THOUSAND UNCONSCIOUS EVENTS, TASKS AND RESPONSIBILITIES THAT SEEMED EASY AND HARMLESS ON THE SURFACE BUT THAT EACH, ONE AFTER THE OTHER, USED A SMALL PORTION OF OUR PRECIOUS LIFE."

-WAYNE MULLER

We were created to rest and, one way or another—be it sickness, be it illness, be it mental illness—your body will rest. I would recommend you "remember the Sabbath" and keep it holy. So, how do we do that? For those of you who are like me and have a hard time slowing down, here are some practical tips:

1. Schedule your Sabbath

Here is a rule of life: if you don't schedule it, it won't happen. Life goes fast, and the older you get, the faster it goes. I remember being a teenager and adults telling me that high school goes fast, and then getting married and my parents telling me that married life goes fast, and now being a parent and older parents telling me that parenting life goes fast too. All of them were right.

Life goes quickly, and if you are not intentional about scheduling time to breathe—time to rest—it will not happen.

I also want to clarify that a day off and a Sabbath are not the same thing. Sabbath is not a day to catch up on the laundry, mow the grass, and knock out a project, unless those things refresh your soul. The Sabbath is a day for rest and worship. Find things that make you feel refreshed and alive and do those things.

For my wife and me, Mondays are our Sabbath. On those days, I do my best to leave my phone upstairs and be present with the family. No emails, no texts, no phone calls. Just rest and worship. We play together, are thankful together, pray together, and take naps. It's a day to refresh for the rest of the week.

Schedule a weekly Sabbath day, small Sabbath moments throughout the day, and then a Sabbath break somewhere in the year. We need rest; schedule it in.

But here is the reality: you will never be *ready* to stop. Just stop.

The emails never end, and the calls never stop. Just make a plan, stick to it, and rest.

> *While Sabbath can refer to a single day of the week, Sabbath can also be a far-reaching, revolutionary tool for cultivating those precious human qualities that grow only in time.*[15]

2. Find what gives you rest

To piggyback on something I touched on a moment ago, you need to be able to identify what refreshes you and what drains you. Do the things that refresh you on the Sabbath.

For me, the gym makes me feel accomplished and rested. For my wife, the gym makes her feel exhausted. So, on Mondays, when our son takes a nap, I go to the gym, and she goes and crafts something. Why? Because we are unique individuals and find refreshment in different ways.

What brings refreshment for you? If you don't know, take some time to figure it out.

Today is a normal workday for me. As a pastor, workdays consist of meetings, counseling, message prepping, team building, emails, planning—a myriad of things. Today, I had a couple come in, and one of them is learning to cope with depression. During our meeting, I explained, as we've discussed, that our mental health is like a bank. Banks have deposits and withdrawals.

If we withdraw more than we deposit, we are in trouble.

Every time we take a Sabbath rest, settling into those things that refresh our souls, we are making deposits. Throughout the course of life, withdrawals are made. We must make sure there is something to withdraw.

> *Every person needs to take one day away. A day in which one consciously separates the past from the future. Jobs, family, employers, and friends can exist one day without any one of us, and if our egos permit us to confess, they could exist eternally in our absence. Each person deserves a day away in which no problems are confronted, no solutions searched for. Each of us needs to withdraw from the cares which will not withdraw from us.*[16]

3. Slow down and declutter

This sounds pretty straightforward, and it is. We need to slow down the pace of our lives. Do we need to go over the speed limit every time we drive? Do we need to switch lanes into the one that seems the fastest? Do we need to switch lines at the grocery store because your clerk looks like the sloth from *Zootopia*? I would say no. Prioritize your life around rest, around a relaxed pace of life.

John Mark Comer's book *The Ruthless Elimination of Hurry* changed my life. He says in it:

> We live with chronically unsatisfied desires. Like an itch that no matter how many times you scratch doesn't go away. No matter how much we see, do, buy, sell, eat, drink, experience, visit, etc., we always want more.[17]

We hurry, and we also hoard. If we do not declutter the things we really don't need, we will waste our time trying to acquire the new, better version of those things. *Declutter* means ridding yourself of things that cost a surplus of time, money, and mental bandwidth.

At some point, we need to sit back, be thankful for who we are and what we have been given, and rest. Stop striving; stop the lust for more things; just be. Slow down, skim off the excess, and declutter your life. Again, from John Mark Comer:

> *Both sin and busyness have the exact same effect—they cut you off from your connection to God, to other people, and even to your own soul.*[18]

God, in His infinite love for humanity, has gifted us with a Sabbath—a time to rest, recharge, and reflect on the beauty of life. Let us not despise the gift before us. The Sabbath was

made for man; let's be thankful and structure our lives around
the divine rhythm of the Sabbath.

CHAPTER 10

WHAT GOES UP MUST COME DOWN

The human being is a self-propelled automaton entirely under the control of external influences. Willful and predetermined though they appear, his actions are governed not from within, but from without. He is like a float tossed about by the waves of a turbulent sea.

—Nikola Tesla

Legend has it that one day an apple fell from a tree, and curiosity was sparked in the mind of Sir Isaac Newton. What force pulls objects down? Why does something dropped always make its way to the earth? Newton continued to observe and hypothesize. Eventually, in 1687, he published his theory of gravity, demonstrating it mathematically.[1] "What goes up must come down", Newton declared.

The law of gravity governs life as we know it on planet earth. We all know this; we experience this daily. Even the struggle of many of us, weight gain, is simply a measurement of the pull of gravity. Losing weight is losing as much gravitational pull as possible. I would know—I may or may not have a well-rounded dad bod coming into full swing. The year 2020 wasn't a great year for a six-pack.

Laws rule and reign over life as we know it. The law of gravity, Newton's first law of motion, Newton's second law of motion, the law of conservation of mass, and the law of conservation of energy are a few that steer the proverbial rudder of the universe.

Other laws, spiritual in nature, I would argue—such as the law of reciprocity, also known as *karma*, sometimes expressed in the words, "What goes around comes around"—hold just as much weight. God has instituted certain laws that have the power to alter our lives for the better if we leverage them for our benefit.

Staying with the example of the law of reciprocity, are you harnessing this law to your benefit? You reap what you sow. So, are you sowing generously with pure motives for the welfare of those who bear the image of the Almighty? I would also argue the law of reciprocity has ramifications on your mental health.

Sow good, reap good.

Love well, be loved well.

Create community for others, receive life-giving community
yourself.

What goes out must come back.

What goes up must come down.

Throughout Scripture, there is another law, if you will—another
concept that governs and oftentimes determines the quality of
life we experience. I call it the law of input. This law could be
summarized like this:

The health of our heart determines the course of our lives.

What we allow to affect and infect our hearts will determine the
outflow of our lives. Music isn't really just music, media isn't
really just media, and relationships aren't really just
relationships. They are all influences; stimuli, that have the
ability to propel you into your destiny or deter you from a
preferable future. The Old Testament declares this truth; Jesus
declares this truth; the apostles declare this truth: input
determines output.

All of our lives illustrate this truth to some degree. As I type this
chapter, I am sitting on my couch on a brisk Monday morning
in October. The results of my typing are the results of my input.
The letter a, comes up because my hunt-and-peck typing
strikes the letter a. When I inevitably run to Target for
something my wife requires later today, I will be able to get

there because I input gas into the car. I put my foot on the accelerator, and the result of that input is motion.

Input determines output. We all innately know this law is in effect, because cause and effect are all around us. Yet, many times, we play the victim, refusing to take responsibility for our inputs, resulting in detrimental outputs.

My wife and I frequently have conversations with young men and women looking for the all-too-elusive phenomenon the human race calls *love*. They typically have a glimmer in their eye, and their cheeks turn a little rosy as they talk about Mr. or Ms. Right. This perfect person, this buffet of manliness or Proverbs 31 woman—whom they met on Tinder or in the club or in some dive bar at three AM when they had way too much to drink—has all the "right" qualities and leaves their hearts aflutter. The sound of their voice is like the whisper of the gods; cupid has gotten ahold of them this time. Unfortunately, oftentimes, there is a look of dismay plastered across their face when we reveal that there is a good chance this certain "totally perfect" individual may be in this relationship for the wrong reasons, based on the meat market where they met.

My wife and I have had this same conversation multiple times about multiple "perfect people" with some of these individuals. Like clockwork, these relationships implode when the not-so-perfect characteristics lurking in the "totally perfect" person come to light. At the end of the day, as hard as it is for them to hear, there is only one common denominator between all of the different "perfect" people. Can you guess what it is?

Ding, ding, ding! It's them. Their input is determining their output. Their dating habits—where they look for love and the decisions they are making—are bringing them less-than-stellar candidates for love.

I use this example to illustrate a simple point. Again: decisions determine results. What you put into something determines what you get out of it. The same is true of what we allow to influence and sway us. What we allow into our hearts, into our minds, and into our souls directly correlates to the quality of life we experience. To put a spin on Sir Isaac Newton, "What goes in must come out." When we discuss mental health and becoming mentally and emotionally healthy, we must realize how vital input is to output.

Guard Your Heart

In Proverbs, Solomon lays out this principle in a beautiful way. I want us to read it in multiple translations, so it really sticks. Proverbs says it this way, in two different translations:

> Above all else, guard your heart, for everything you do flows from it. (Proverbs 4:23 NIV)

> Guard your heart above all else, for it determines the course of your life. (Proverbs 4:23 NLT)

THE
HEALTH
OF YOUR
HEART
DETERMINES
THE
DIRECTION
OF YOUR
LIFE

Solomon pleads with his audience to prioritize the guarding of their hearts. The heart was believed by the Jews of the Ancient Near East to be the core, the center, of the human being. The heart was the seat of the emotions, the place from which the mind and the will stemmed. The epicenter of personality and personhood found its origin in the heart. The core, the center, is to be guarded "above all else." The phrase "above all else", or as some translations put it, "with all diligence", is the Hebrew phrase *mikol-mishmar*. *Mishmar* is often used in Scripture to describe a prison or a place of confinement. In fact, in Genesis 40:3, Joseph is in prison, and the word used to describe Joseph in "custody" is *mishmar*.

So, get this picture Solomon is painting: Wisdom screams for us to guard our hearts—the core, the seat of our minds, will, and emotions—as if they were in custody. The heart is so vital to the quality of life we experience that we are to prioritize its protection like prisons prioritize the lockup of their inhabitants.

The question would be, Why? Why is it so important to guard that area of our lives? Glad you asked. Let's focus on Solomon's follow-up comment:

> Proverbs 4:23 NLT
>
> Guard your heart above all else, for it determines the course of your life.

Read that again, slowly. Let it sink in.

The health of your heart determines the direction of your life.

The health of your heart—your mind, will, and emotions—determines the course of your life. If your heart is unhealthy, your life will be unhealthy. If your heart is broken, your life will be broken. If your heart is perverse, your life will be surrounded by perversion. Our hearts affect every area of our lives, so their protection is vital. What we allow to affect and infect our core steers our lives.

Think of the water in a reservoir. Whatever spills into that water flows out to those who use the water and that in turn affects the quality and purity of the water when it is used.

Again, read what Solomon wrote:

> Above all else, guard your heart, for everything you do flows from it. (Proverbs 4:23 NIV)

For *EVERYTHING* you do, the course of your life *flows* from your heart. It's a river. Your life, your future, your relationships, and your mental health flow from the health of your heart. What we allow to influence and infiltrate our heart is a really, really big deal.

Jesus and the Heart

Often, people have misunderstood what Jesus came and taught. He did not come to discount the law God gave to Moses. Scripture is clear that He came to fulfill the righteous requirements of the law given to Israel. The law was given as a mirror to show humanity how broken and depraved we are. If we could keep every precept perfectly, we could earn salvation. But we can't—not in our own strength and ability. Only God can do that. Which is why Jesus, fully God, fully man, accomplished what we could not.

Jesus actually raises the bar in His teachings. The law simply focuses on actions; Jesus focuses on our hearts and our intentions. In the famous Sermon on the Mount, Jesus realigns the expectation of man with the priorities of heaven.

> Do not think that I have come to abolish the Law or the Prophets; I have not come to abolish them but to fulfill them…. You have heard that it was said to the people long ago, "You shall not murder, and anyone who murders will be subject to judgment." But I tell you that anyone who is angry with a brother or sister will be subject to judgment…. You have heard that it was said, "You shall not commit adultery." But I tell you that anyone who looks at a woman lustfully has already committed adultery with her in his heart. (Matthew 5:17, 21–22, 27–28 NIV)

We frequently see Jesus say, "You have heard…, but I tell you." In other words, here's what you expect, but here are the actual priorities of heaven. What we see is clear: the heart, the intentions, the motivation, the core of the person matters more than the actions, because the heart informs actions. If the heart changes, the actions inevitably change. Jesus is always going after the heart of the person, because the heart determines the direction of life. The heart determines the flow of life. Change the heart, change the life.

In the same teaching, Jesus again speaks to the importance of heart health:

> A good man brings good things out of the good stored up in his heart, and an evil man brings evil things out of the evil stored up in his heart. For the mouth speaks what the heart is full of. (Luke 6:45 NIV)

Jesus is reiterating that the life lived is the direct result of the quality of the contents of the heart. In fact, He even goes so far as to say the content of our speech is directed by the overflow of whatever our heart is full of. If we have an issue being angry, or bitter, or negative, we do not have a filter issue—we have a heart condition. If we can't control our tongues, it's because we haven't guarded our hearts. Our speech is a direct reflection of the health of our hearts.

A huge part of my job is meeting with people. Often, when I sit down with people, I will just ask them some kind of open-ended question that lends itself to some degree of vulnerability and then let them speak for as long as possible. In listening to what is communicated, I can tell where their heart is. I can tell how their mind, will, and emotions are doing by allowing them simply to speak uninterrupted. Speech is a reflection of the soul. The condition of the heart leaks.

If I were to sit down with you, what would the content of your speech be?

Are you thankful?
Are you gracious?

Are you speaking well of others?

Or

Are you gossiping?
Are you negative?
Are you sarcastic to an unhealthy degree?

The content of your speech directly correlates to the health of your heart, and the health of your heart directs the course of your life. Jesus knew this, and He went after heart change. Again, the health of your heart matters. Solomon said to guard it; Jesus spoke to the importance of it; it appears we should value it.

Influences and Stimuli

Since our entire life is influenced by the health of our hearts, that includes our mental health. What we allow to sway our hearts has repercussions on the quality of the mental lives we live. In guarding our hearts and being choosy about what we allow to wiggle its way in, we are guarding our mental well-being. So, what do we need to guard against?

Great question.

What we are going to discuss can be seen as legalism or some kind of dead religion. I want to be clear: obviously, sin is an issue we must deal with, but what we are talking about here is not necessarily just sin; more specifically, we are talking about what infects and affects you. In talking about the life of faith we are to live, the writer of Hebrews says this:

> Therefore, since we are surrounded by such a huge crowd of witnesses to the life of faith, let us strip off *every weight that slows us down*, especially the sin that so easily trips us up. And let us run with endurance the race God has set before us. (Hebrews 12:1 NLT, emphasis mine)

Notice the writer of Hebrews makes a clear delineation in the things that can jeopardize our walk of faith. There is sin, and then there are weights. There is sin, and then there are things that hinder. Sin is universal—sin crosses all boundaries and applies to all of us. Murder is wrong for everyone. Lying and cheating are wrong for everyone. Sin is universally, invariably applied to all humanity.

Weights, on the other hand, are personal. Maybe on their own, they are not sinful, but for you or for me, they are a problem. We have to know the things that hinder and pollute our hearts. We have to throw off the things that hinder. We have to throw off the weights that will slow us in the race that lies before us. Taking proper inventory of our hearts is vital to find out what stimuli are detrimental to us operating at full capacity. There may be things that affect you that don't affect me. There may be areas that my spirit is sensitive to, but God has wired you differently. With that being said, let's chat about some stimuli— some influences—that require discretion, so we can properly guard our hearts and have a life marked by mental stability.

1. Relationships

Since I was a wee little chap in kids' church, I have heard, "Show me your friends, and I'll show you your future." As a kid, I grimaced and rolled my eyes with such force every time an adult uttered that phrase, that I'm surprised they didn't stick.

I'm not *that* vulnerable.

Yes, yes you are.

> Do not be deceived: "Bad company ruins good morals." (1 Corinthians 15:33 ESV)

Paul is making a strong claim. Bad company corrupts good character. In other words, "Show me your friends, and I will show you your future." Notice, Paul says, "Don't be deceived." He has to say "Don't be deceived" because humans are often deceived into believing that those they hang around—those they allow to influence their lives—don't really affect them. That is foolish; it's deception; it's stupid. Now, I am not saying you and three Christians friends who all listen to K-LOVE, only wear Not of This World T-shirts, and take turns singing "Lord, I Lift Your Name On High" need to reject the world and refuse to love on broken people who have yet to believe in Jesus. That would be contrary to Scripture. What I am saying is that those closest to you need to champion who you are in Christ and not deter you. They need to be people who remind you of the high call of God, who are full of faith, who live generously, and who are constantly looking for the beauty in people and refuse to settle for critique. Those closest to you need to push you toward Jesus.

Maybe, just maybe, the reason you can't seem to get out of a cycle of negative thinking is that the three people closest to you are chronically negative. Maybe, just maybe, the reason you aren't thriving even in the midst of chronic depression is that the closest relationships in your life are doom and gloom and lack any measure of faith. Maybe you can't seem to win your battle with anxiety because the people closest to you are always in a hurry, frequently late, and can't keep their lives organized, and it's messing with your mental health. We need people—the right people. We need to be selective about who we allow to influence us. Those closest to us should be pushing us toward health and pushing us to fall more in love with Jesus.

2. Media

Very few things are as impactful as the media we consume. The dictionary definition of *media* is "the main means of mass communication." By its very definition, the goal of media is to communicate something. So, the question we must ask is, *What* is being communicated? Are we surrounding ourselves with God-honoring, godly media or media that is peddling mass hysteria and fear? We must be selective with what media and how much media we allow into our hearts.

Now, when I say *media*, there are many modes of communication that make up the broad term *media*. The music we listen to, the videos we watch, and the news stations we tune in to all make up media intake. When I reference guarding what media we consume, I am speaking of all the above. Earlier, I made a statement that holds true:

Music is not just music.
Movies are not just movies.
News is not just news.

They are all stimuli that we allow into the eye-and-ear gates of our hearts. Garbage in, garbage out. Disrespect in, disrespect out. Paranormal activity in, demon possession out... I'm just kidding. But seriously, don't watch those movies. Let's talk about all those for a moment.

Music. Very few things house the power that music houses. Throughout Scripture, we see the medium of music being utilized to glorify God, go before the army to win battles, and even deter demonic spirits. When King Saul is being tormented by an evil spirit, it is David playing his harp as a minstrel before the Lord that causes Saul's agony to cease. God commands Jehoshaphat to send the worshippers first, declaring, "You are good, and Your love endures," in the face of certain defeat, in order to witness God's supernatural triumph. We see the ministry of music used by the prophets to usher in the presence and voice of God. Music is powerful and can be wielded for both good and evil.

The music we allow ourselves to listen to fills the container of our hearts. Much of the content of music today is demonic in nature, belittling and degrading to women, and encourages violence and a spirit of rebellion. That's not good for your heart, thus not good for your mind and mental health. It's not just about listening to a beat—music is a medium for communication. So, what are you allowing yourself to listen to? What is being communicated? Guard your heart.

Film. I love film as an art form. I used to film short videos and skits quite a bit when I was younger. In high school, a couple of my dumb friends and I were handed the reigns of the student rallies. I'm not sure who thought that was a good idea. We would frequently dream up videos to communicate whatever the theme of the rally was supposed to be. Very few outlets can communicate as deeply to someone's soul as film. In film, we can identify with characters and in so doing, allow their story to become our story, their thoughts to become our thoughts. Film has literally influenced nations.

For example, in 1905, a novel titled *The Clansman* was written by Thomas Dixon Jr. The concept of the novel, which is part history and part fiction, is the glorification of Southern heritage and demonization of African Americans. Black Americans are shown as barbaric, preying on innocent white women to fulfill their "sexual deviance." The KKK is shown to be the heroes, riding in to save the day and rescue the damsels in distress from the evil black men. The novel was first adapted into a play, and then into an uncompleted film in 1911. After shopping the film around, *The Clansman* was released and then renamed *The Birth of a Nation* in 1915. The film spread like wildfire, with showings even hosted in the White House by Woodrow Wilson, who proclaimed, "It's like writing history with lightning. My only regret is that it is all so terribly true."[2] Many historians credit *The Birth of a Nation* with the reemergence of the KKK, and new rituals presented in the film, such as cross burning, became commonplace in the Jim Crow South.

I take you on this brief history lesson to show that film has the ability to influence and sway culture. A racist terrorist organization found rebirth, largely due to the influence of a film. We are naïve if we believe that film intake—be it Netflix, movies, or primetime TV shows—doesn't affect the core of who we are. Something is being communicated through what we watch. Is what you watch adding value or polluting? Guard your heart.

News. There was a day in the not-too-distant past when the news was trustworthy. Journalists sought to report accurate, credible stories, rather than seeking to win the race of "Who was first?" Today, it seems the goal is not accuracy; the details will be cleaned up after the fact.

Case in point: the tragic, untimely death of Kobe Bryant. Early in 2020, Kobe Bryant passed away in a helicopter crash. I remember the moment well. I was sitting in the front row in the middle of a church service, when my phone began to be inundated with texts and alerts. The plethora of differing information about who was on the helicopter and what happened was sickening. Vanessa Bryant, Kobe's wife, found out about her daughter and husband's deaths while getting her nails done, through a TMZ report. How horrific is that? In this instance, it was abundantly clear that news outlets cared little about getting the story correct and lacked any measure of humanity, instead opting for "clickbait" that may or may not have been true.

In our day and age, we consume copious amounts of news, and much of that is bad news. Let me be clear in saying that if you consume hours of news on a daily basis, you are going to have issues with anxiety. I've heard it said that bad news sells, and the ratings prove that to be true. Bad news is everywhere, and fake news is everywhere. News with the goal of making money is irresponsibly aiding the split of the country, and the split of families over minutiae. It doesn't matter what side of the aisle you are on; the goal of news is to make money not guard the truth or your mental health. Neither CNN nor Fox News is concerned about your anxiety levels. We must regulate the frequency with which we consume news. Guard your heart.

What we allow ourselves to consume has implications for our hearts.

Just Need Some Help?

While we are talking about input and output, let's talk about medication and counseling briefly. There is a ridiculous stigma about taking medication for mental illness. Somehow, those who take medication are often viewed as irresponsible or mentally weak. Allow me to be blunt: that's stupid and hypocritical. If your liver wasn't functioning properly, you would seek medical advice and proceed accordingly. If your kidneys were not operating at 100 percent, you wouldn't sit back and suffer in silence. Your brain is an organ that needs to be cared for; seek professional medical advice and proceed accordingly.

Both my wife and I are on antidepressants and antianxiety medication. For a long time, we just tried to pull ourselves up by our bootstraps and get better. It didn't work. We both got to a place where we wanted to die and couldn't function.

Get the help you need. Go to the doctor. If you need to take medication, do it. Maybe God is choosing to use the wisdom of modern medicine to heal your invisible illness. Taking medicine is not a lack of faith; on the contrary, it's wisdom. Heal up—get the right input.

It is vital to seek medical expertise when learning to heal and thrive with mental illness. God, in His creativity and grace, granted humanity the ability to create and develop technology. Modern medicine is a common grace. Don't resist the grace of God because of an archaic stigma. Seek help.

Part of seeking the right help is finding a good counselor. I am a firm believer in counseling. Everyone—and I mean everyone—needs a good counselor. Life comes complete with high highs and really low lows, and often we do not know how to process all that life throws at us. Good counselors can help see what you cannot see and teach you how to process what you do not currently have the skills to process.

In California, no one knows how to drive, and everyone is overly rushed and aggressive on the road. I try to even things out, be a good Christian, and use my blinker when changing lanes. I'll flip that little blinker switch, get ready to change lanes, look over my shoulder, and BAM! Becky over there is camping right in that little blind spot that my mirrors can't see. It's disgraceful, dishonorable; deplorable even. She doesn't deserve to have the privilege of driving. Don't camp in people's blind spots.

Blind spots are annoying when driving but even more annoying in life. Every person on planet earth has blind spots. Spouses are great blind-spot detectors and so are counselors. Humans are creatures of habit, and we often don't realize our habits can become detrimental to our mental health. In order to live in a reality complete with solid mental health, we often need the input of a professional counselor. They are trained to discern blind spots and help you to manage them. If you or someone you love deals with any variation of invisible illness, get counseling.

Again, input determines output. What you allow to influence and infiltrate your heart—the center of who you are—will have repercussions on your mental health.

> Above all else, guard your heart, for everything you do flows from it. (Proverbs 4:23 niv)

Above all else, guard your heart. The quality of life you experience is a direct reflection of the content of your heart. Are you careful about what you allow to affect and infect your heart, or is it a consumer free-for-all?

Thriving with mental illness requires a great deal of intentionality spiritually, mentally, and practically. Guard your heart. What goes up must come down; what goes in must come out. The health of your heart determines the course of your life.

CHAPTER 11

REST FOR YOUR SOUL

> *He that takes his cares on himself loads himself in vain with an uneasy burden. I will cast my cares on God; He has bidden me; they cannot burden Him.*
>
> —Joseph Hall

A few chapters ago, I mentioned an internship program I did right after high school. It was two of the best years of my life. The program was what I lovingly refer to as God Bootcamp— part Bible college, part hard labor, part hands-on ministry training. I loved it.

In an effort to create a bond between the students, within the first two weeks of the program, we set off to hike what we were told is the second tallest mountain in the continental U.S., Mount Langley. Before we left, we were given massive hiking packs and loaded them down with tents, propane tanks, freeze-dried food, and whatever else Pastor Raymond deemed necessary. Pastor Raymond is one of the most well-rounded individuals I have ever had the pleasure of knowing. He's a pastor, an entrepreneur, and a politician. He's equally loving and equally "I will throat punch you." For years, he ran a business taking people into the great outdoors and summiting mountains, so we all felt a degree of safety.

The day we set off; we were excited; we were ready to go. Bear Grylls highlights played through my mind, as testosterone coursed through my veins. I'll never forget the moment I strapped on my seventy-five-pound pack and set off for what would be over twenty miles of hiking. The hike wasn't bad, but the pack was brutal. Your lower back starts to give out, the side straps rub your hips raw, and your shoulders go numb. The weight was horrific.

Halfway through, some of the other students were not able to continue with their packs, so some of us took on additional packs. Now I had all of my weight mixed with somebody else's weight. There were moments when the pain and the exhaustion were excruciating. Humans weren't designed to carry that much physical weight for an extended amount of time.

What I just described above is how some of us feel as we battle through our invisible illness. There is a weight that feels unbearable. We proverbially trek through the wilderness, desiring to summit the peak of life, while carrying our own weight of mental illness comingled with the baggage of others.

Some of us are determined to carry the weight without help.
Grin and bear it.
We got this.
We can brave it alone.

How's that going for you? How does the weight feel? How does it feel to be the Lone Ranger without Tonto? Batman with no Robin? Braving mental illness alone, carrying the weight of what is going through your mind as if it were no big deal.

It is a big deal.

It's baggage you were not designed to carry.

I imagine you look like I must have looked on that mountain: doing your best to just move one step at a time without collapsing under the weight of the baggage you carry. Exhausted but thinking, *Just one more step.* Let me ask again, how is that working for you?

Law or Weight

Before Jesus stepped onto the scene, the Jews were burdened by hundreds of laws exacerbated by commentaries upon those laws. The Pharisees—the teachers of religious law—not only expected every man, woman, and child to keep the 631 laws prescribed in the Old Testament, they expected them to observe the extra laws added for good measure as well. The teachers of religious law built "safeguards" around the laws to ensure no one could come close to infringing upon them (thus the Sabbath debacle).

Imagine what it must feel like to wake up every morning to the gnawing reality that in order to maintain any measure of holiness, you must keep hundreds of laws and hundreds of guidelines upon those laws. Brutal, unfathomable. This whole dilemma was what infuriated Jesus.

As you read through the Gospels, you quickly realize Jesus welcomed the broken and the sinful but lectured and firmly rebuked the religious leaders. The religious leaders were overburdening the people He loved. They were coercing individuals into a lifestyle that God never intended them to live. A lifestyle constricted by man-made dos and don'ts is not the life—and life to the full—Jesus came to offer.

In the Gospel of Luke, Jesus is invited to a Pharisee's home for dinner. Jesus accepts the invitation but neglects to observe the Jewish ritual of handwashing. This catches the Pharisee off guard, and Jesus begins a tirade of "woe-to-you" decrees, including a rebuke for weighing down the people He so loved.

> Jesus replied, "And you experts in the law, woe to you, because you load people down with burdens they can hardly carry, and you yourselves will not lift one finger to help them." (Luke 11:46 NIV)

Weight, exhaustion, and no hope for a successful life in God are not what our Creator intended for us.

Come to Me

A rabbi would develop his own interpretations and practical applications of the Scripture, called his "yoke." The disciples of the rabbi would cling to their teacher's yoke and dedicate their lives to learning, understanding, and rightly applying the yoke of their rabbi.

The yoke of the Pharisees was difficult to live out. It was cumbersome; it was heavy.

In one of my favorite verses of Scripture, Jesus addresses this idea and shows a stark contrast of who He is in comparison to dead religion:

> Come to Me, all you who are weary and burdened, and I will give you rest. Take My yoke upon you and learn from Me, for I am gentle and humble in heart, and you will find rest for your souls. (Matthew 11:28–29 NIV)

Jesus is offering a yoke, a set of teachings and interpretations, quite different from that of the teachers of religious law. He offers a yoke not based on our works but based on His finished work on the cross. He offers a yoke marked by grace rather than our ability to keep man-made rules. He offers a yoke that allows us to lean on His strength rather than depending on our own.

MATTHEW 11:28-29 NIV

"COME TO ME, ALL YOU WHO ARE WEARY AND BURDENED, AND I WILL GIVE YOU REST. TAKE MY YOKE UPON YOU AND LEARN FROM ME, FOR I AM GENTLE AND HUMBLE IN HEART, AND YOU WILL FIND REST FOR YOUR SOULS."

All of us buy into some yoke. All of us are living by and applying some version of Scripture interpretation. Regardless of whether we are applying the teachings of Jesus or of atheism, we all buy into some yoke. The question is:

What yoke are you adhering to?

Is it heavy and burdensome or light and easy?

Many of us who deal with variations of mental illness have a heavy yoke—a feeling of exhaustion under the weight of our condition. We've bought into believing that our mental illness is ours and ours alone to carry.

That's a lie. That isn't what Jesus intended for us to experience. His invitation is simple:

> Come to Me, all you who are weary and burdened, and I will give you rest.

The invitation from Jesus is an invitation to unload cumbersome burdens and receive rest.

My Realization

Growing up as the firstborn, I felt a lot of pressure, which I am sure was self-inflicted, to have it all together. I felt pressure to "be enough", to be strong and self-reliant. Those feelings leaked into the way I handled my mental health. For years, I suffered in silence, unwilling to let any inkling of weakness see the light of day.

No one can know I'm struggling.

No one can know what is going through my head.
As we have discussed, the results weren't great. My depression and anxiety grew worse, and I started to lean into suicidal ideation.

One day, I finally got to a point where I stopped caring what people thought. *Go ahead and reject me. Go ahead and think I'm weak. I can't do this alone.*

I spent extended time in the secret place—just me and Jesus. I would sit at the piano and cry out to God, bearing my soul, my frustrations, my fears, and my doubts. The more I played, the more I wept. The more I sang, the more my soul felt the rest Jesus promised. In that space—that scary, vulnerable space—God met me. His presence became my refuge. I experienced the peace that the Prince of Peace can offer. In His presence, there is fulness of joy.

It wasn't until I let others carry my burdens and laid all I am at the feet of Jesus that a degree of rest came. I'm not completely healed of my invisible illness. I still deal with bouts of depression, and my social anxiety can be debilitating for sure. But I have learned the rest my soul craves can only be found in His presence. I can't carry the weight of my mental illness, so I come, weary and heavy burdened. I allow my Savior to teach me. I take His yoke upon me.

At the end of the day, we do the best we can to be good stewards of what is in our hands. We stay healthy to the best of our ability, eliminate triggers, do self-inventory, and remove as many obstacles as possible, and then we trust God with the results. We may never see 100 percent freedom from the mental illness we experience on this side of eternity, but we "pray until." We believe until. We are thankful for good seasons and bad seasons. And we rest in His presence.

We sit at the feet of Jesus.
He is gentle and humble in heart.

So, friends, are you carrying this weight alone? Are you stuck in rugged individualism, braving the recesses of your mind alone? Let me ask again, How is that going for you?

Our Savior, the Man of Sorrows, acquainted with deepest grief, has issued an invitation to you. He has invited you to come and find rest. Jesus uses the Greek verb *anapauo* for rest. *Anapauo* means "to refresh or give an intermission from labor." We all need a bit of a break and some refreshing. The refreshing we all desire can only come from Jesus. So, come to Him. Allow Him to define how you live and move and breathe. Allow Him to take the weight you have been carrying. Allow Him to unload the burdensome weight.

In John 14, Jesus is speaking to the disciples, explaining that He is going to depart soon, but He is going to leave the Holy Spirit, the Advocate. Then He makes a promise to His disciples, a promise that holds true for those of us who have made Jesus our Lord:

> Peace I leave with you; my peace I give you. I do not give to you as the world gives. Do not let your

hearts be troubled and do not be afraid. (John 14:27 NIV)

This is a promise for you and for me, for all who have submitted the whole of their lives to Christ. The peace He promises can be translated to wholeness. Jesus promises wholeness, even in our imperfection. There is a peace, a wholeness, that is present even in the midst of hardship, uncertainty, and calamity. Life may not be perfect; it may come complete with seasons we do not understand, as we exclaim, WHY? Yet, through it all, there can be peace. There can be wholeness.

Boats and Storms

In the Gospel of Mark, we get a beautiful picture of what life as a follower of Jesus looks like. One day, Jesus tells His disciples He wants to hop in a boat and go to the other side of the lake. So, the disciples, following the lead of their rabbi, jump into the boat, hoist the sails, and set off. Jesus is apparently a little drowsy from continuous ministry and heads to the stern for a little catnap. Scripture apparently wants us to know the level of comfort Jesus is experiencing, because it details that He is sleeping on a pillow. Comfortable—not a care in the world.

On the deck, there are plenty of cares to be had. The weather has gone south quickly, the skies are black, and the wind is blowing. The NIV details the storm as a "furious squall." Water is pouring into the boat, and the disciples—who, by the way, are experienced fishermen—are afraid for their lives. They think *this* is the end. They can see the light at the end of the tunnel. Their lives are flashing before their eyes. Death is imminent.

Filled to the brim with fear, the disciples go and wake up Jesus from His beauty sleep and exclaim:

> Teacher, don't You care if we drown? (Mark 4:38b niv)

The Savior, whom they have seen heal the sick, cast out demons, and move in power, is asleep in their darkest hour. Their go-to thought is questioning His caring nature.

Surely, He wouldn't allow *this* to happen if He cared. Surely, we would not have to go through *this* if He cared. Surely.

We have all been there, doubting the compassion of God in the midst of navigating hardship. Forgetting His provision amid lack. Overlooking His faithfulness in the midst of what seems impossible. Questioning His reckless love while dealing with overwhelming depression and anxiety. The Master is asleep on the job, while I'm on the deck battling for my life. If we were to take an honest moment to analyze our thought processes, we'd have to admit we've all been there and will probably be there again.

But Jesus isn't afraid of our doubts. He isn't taken aback by our lapses in faithfulness. When we are faithless, He is *faithful*. He isn't afraid of the disciples' questions. He reminds them of their lack of faith and how they need to remember who He is, and He rebukes the waves and storms in an instant.

Jesus has power and dominion over the whole of creation, which includes our mental well-being. One word from Jesus, and depression and anxiety must relinquish control of our minds. He is the same yesterday, today, and forever. He is the Good Physician; He is our healer.

Now, that doesn't mean every storm is calmed in an instant. Yes, He heals, but there is an element of mystery involved in experiencing that healing. Healing doesn't always look like we think it should. He may heal through counseling and medication. He may supernaturally heal in an instant, or He may choose to heal when we pass on from this life into eternity. We pray, asking God to intervene, yet declaring, "He is still good, even if He doesn't."

When we read this narrative in Mark, we tend to focus on the weather-altering declaration.

"PEACE, BE STILL!"

Wow—climactic, epic, amazing.

Yet, oftentimes, it doesn't feel applicable. It serves to remind us that Jesus, the Son of God, is omnipotent, all-powerful. He created the weather systems and rules over them. Yet our prayers often seemingly go unanswered. I still deal with mental illness daily and have done my best to serve Jesus. Where is my "PEACE, BE STILL"?

We focus on the massive miracle while ignoring the practical, encouraging love of God displayed in this story. Notice, during the waves, in the midst of the rain and the fear and the doubt, Jesus never leaves the boat.

He is present.
He is near.
He is with them.
He is in the boat in the midst of the storm.

So, it is with us. Our illnesses may not vanish overnight—our prayers may seem unanswered at times—yet through it all, there is an ever-present Prince of Peace in our boat. Run to Him, throw your cares at His feet, and allow His peace and presence to become your refuge in the midst of uncertainty.

Let me leave you with this encouragement from the apostle Paul:

> Be anxious for nothing, but in everything by prayer and supplication, with thanksgiving, let your requests be made known to God; and the peace of God, which surpasses all understanding, will guard your hearts and minds through Christ Jesus. (Philippians 4:6–7 nkjv)

Be anxious for nothing, yet bring everything to the feet of Jesus. This is Paul's way of reminding us of the invitation of Jesus:

Come to Me, all you who are weary and burdened, and I will give you rest. Take My yoke upon you and learn from Me, for I am gentle and humble in heart, and you will find rest for your souls. (Matthew 11:28–29 NIV)

Rest is available in the midst of hardship. Peace is available in the midst of confusion. Let us steward well what we have been given, while clinging to King Jesus for peace. Only Jesus can grant us "peace that surpasses understanding."

Our Champion, our King, our Lord has left us with peace. Let us run to our Savior, lay our burdens at His feet, take His yoke, and allow His peace to wash over our minds and souls. There is rest for our minds. We don't have to settle for allowing invisible illness to control the outcome of who we are. The finished work of the cross affords us the mind of Christ. His mind has no anxiety or confusion or fear. His mind is filled with love, joy, peace, patience, kindness, goodness, faithfulness, gentleness, and self-control. That is our inheritance.

We may deal with invisible illness on this earth, but our Savior has the final word. He promises peace and rest, if we will simply come. Let's accept His invitation.

ENDNOTES

Introduction

1. Johnston, Jeremiah J. "Unanswered". 2015.Whitaker House,

CHAPTER 1

1. "Mental Health by the Numbers" NAMI, National Alliance on Mental Illness, Sep. 2019, www.nami.org/mhstats
2. Fox, Maggie. "Major Depression on the Rise among Everyone, New Data Shows." NBCNews.com, NBCUniversal News Group, 11 May 2018, www.nbcnews.com/health/health-news/major-depression-rise-among-everyone-new-data-shows-n873146.

3. "Americans Feel Good About Counseling." Barna Group, www.barna.com/research/americans-feel-good-counseling/.

4. Jesus, the Light of the World, Opens the Eyes of a Man Born Blind." John 9 Commentary - Jesus, the Light of the World, Opens the Eyes of a Man Born Blind - BibleGateway.com, InterVarsity Press., www.biblegateway.com/resources/commentaries/IVP-NT/John/Jesus-Light-World-Opens-Eyes.

5. "Nearly Half of Pastors Have Struggled with Depression." Influence2, Influence Magazine, 9 Nov. 2019, influencemagazine.com/Theory/Nearly-Half-of-Pastors-Have-Struggled-with-Depression.

6. Reeves (PhD, Michael. "Did You Know That Charles Spurgeon Struggled with Depression?" Crossway, Crossway, 24 Feb. 2018, www.crossway.org/articles/did-you-know-that-charles-spurgeon-struggled-with-depression/.

7. Cox, Brandon A. "Can a Pastor Who Struggles With Depression Remain a Pastor?" Ministry Today Magazine, Charisma Media, 20 Sept. 2019, ministrytodaymag.com/leadership/a-pastor-s-heart/26292-can-a-pastor-who-struggles-with-depression-remain-a-pastor.

8. Cox, Brandon. "What You Need to Know About Pastors and Depression." Ministry Today Magazine, Charisma Media, 3 Jan. 2018, ministrytodaymag.com/personal-

growth/24519-what-you-need-to-know-about-pastors-and-depression.

9. Young, Jack. Tozer and Spurgeon on Suffering and Brokenness, 1 May 2019, www.pastorjack.org/?p=2127, emphasis added.

CHAPTER 2

1. Julson, Erica. "11 Signs and Symptoms of Anxiety Disorders." Nutrition, Healthline, 10 April 2018, https://www.healthline.com/nutrition/anxiety-disorder-symptoms

2. Hahn, Lance. "How to Live in Fear". W Publishing Group, 2016.

3. Spurgeon, Charles H. "Psalm 42 Bible Commentary." Psalm 42 Bible Commentary - Charles H. Spurgeon's Treasury of David, Hendrickson Publishers, 1988, www.christianity.com/bible/commentary.php?com=spur &b=19&c=42.

CHAPTER 3

1. McCann, Adam. "2020's Best Coffee Cities in America." WalletHub, 23 Sept. 2020, wallethub.com/edu/best-cities-for-coffee-lovers/23739.

2. "Nature vs. Nurture: Effects on Genes, Mental & Physical Health." MedicineNet, MedicineNet, 17 Dec. 2019,

www.medicinenet.com/nature_vs_nurture_theory_genes
_or_environment/article.htm.

3. Ariel Bar-Sela, Hebbel E. Hoff and Elias Farus, "Moses Maimonides' Two Treatises on the Regimen of Health," Transactions of the American Philosophical Society, ns, 54 (1964), Part 4: 25.

4. Anindita, Adhika. "Understanding the Mental Health and Mental Illness Continuum." The Jakarta Post, The Jakarta Post, 3 Apr. 2018, www.thejakartapost.com/life/2018/04/03/understanding -the-mental-health-and-mental-illness-continuum.html.

5. Bhandari, Smitha. "Causes of Mental Illness." WebMD, WebMD, 30 June 2020, www.webmd.com/mental-health/mental-health-causes-mental-illness#1.

6. "Common Genetic Factors Found in 5 Mental Disorders." National Institutes of Health, U.S. Department of Health and Human Services, 18 May 2013, www.nih.gov/news-events/nih-research-matters/common-genetic-factors-found-5-mental-disorders.

7. Does Mental Illness Run in Families? Rethink Mental Illness, Sept. 2020, www.rethink.org/advice-and-information/carers-hub/does-mental-illness-run-in-families/.

8. "Inheriting Mental Disorders." HealthyChildren.org, American Academy of Pediatrics, 21 Nov. 2015, www.healthychildren.org/English/health-

issues/conditions/emotional-problems/Pages/Inheriting-Mental-Disorders.aspx.

9. Bray, Bethany. "Living with – and beyond – a Family Legacy: Q A with Mariel Hemingway." Counseling Today, AMERICAN COUNSELING ASSOCIATION. , 9 Feb. 2015, ct.counseling.org/2015/02/living-with-and-beyond-a-family-legacy-qa-with-mariel-hemingway/.

10. "What Are the Causes of Mental Illness?" The Kim Foundation, The Kim Foundation, 2020, www.thekimfoundation.org/causes/.

11. Bhandari, Smitha. "Causes of Mental Illness." WebMD, WebMD, 30 June 2020, www.webmd.com/mental-health/mental-health-causes-mental-illness#1.

12. Zimlich, Rachael. "Role of Infectious Disease in Mental Illness Development." Contemporary Pediatrics, Contemporary Pediatrics, 18 Feb. 2019, www.contemporarypediatrics.com/view/role-infectious-disease-mental-illness-development.

13. Sartorius N, Holt RIG, Maj M (eds): Comorbidity of Mental and Physical Disorders. Key Issues Ment Health. Basel, Karger, 2015, vol 179, pp 99–113 (DOI: 10.1159/000365542)

14. Müller, Norbert. "Infectious Diseases and Mental Health." Comorbidity of Mental and Physical Illness: A Selective Review, Department of Psychiatry and Psychotherapy, Ludwig-Maximilian University Munich, 2015, www.karger.com/Article/Pdf/365542.

15. "Frequently Asked Questions about CTE." Frequently Asked Questions about CTE | CTE Center, Boston University Research CTE Center, www.bu.edu/cte/about/frequently-asked-questions/.

16. Hansen, Malene Breusch. "Head Injury Can Cause Mental Illness." ScienceNordic, 3 Jan. 2014, sciencenordic.com/biology-denmark-depression/head-injury-can-cause-mental-illness/1395035.

17. Hansen, Malene Breusch. "Head Injury Can Cause Mental Illness." ScienceNordic, 3 Jan. 2014, sciencenordic.com/biology-denmark-depression/head-injury-can-cause-mental-illness/1395035.

18. "Mental Health Disorders Common Following Mild Head Injury." National Institutes of Health, U.S. Department of Health and Human Services, 30 Jan. 2019, www.nih.gov/news-events/news-releases/mental-health-disorders-common-following-mild-head-injury.

19. Cherry, Kendra. "The Age Old Debate of Nature vs. Nurture." Verywell Mind, About, Inc., 3 June 2020, www.verywellmind.com/what-is-nature-versus-nurture-2795392.

20. National Coalition Against Domestic Violence (2020). Domestic violence. Retrieved from https://assets.speakcdn.com/assets/2497/domestic_violence-2020080709350855.pdf?1596811079991.

21. "Effects of Child Abuse and Neglect for Adult Survivors." Child Family Community Australia, Australian Institute of Family Studies., Jan. 2014,

aifs.gov.au/cfca/publications/effects-child-abuse-and-neglect-adult-survivors.

22. Canadian, Association Mental Health. "Childhood Sexual Abuse: A Mental Health Issue." Heretohelp, BC Partners for Mental Health and Substance Use Information, 2013, www.heretohelp.bc.ca/infosheet/childhood-sexual-abuse-a-mental-health-issue.

23. Roberts, Ron, et al. "The Effects of Child Sexual Abuse in Later Family Life; Mental Health, Parenting and Adjustment of Offspring." Child Abuse & Neglect, Pergamon, 28 Apr. 2004, www.sciencedirect.com/science/article/abs/pii/S014521 3404000808.

24. Keyes, Katherine M, et al. "The Burden of Loss: Unexpected Death of a Loved One and Psychiatric Disorders across the Life Course in a National Study." The American Journal of Psychiatry, U.S. National Library of Medicine, 1 Aug. 2014, www.ncbi.nlm.nih.gov/pmc/articles/PMC4119479/.

25. "How Does Family Life Affect Mental Health?" Mental Health Center, Sylvia Brafman Mental Health Center, 8 June 2017, www.mentalhealthcenter.org/how-does-family-life-affect-mental-health/.

26. "Find out How Parents Affect Their Children's Mental Health!" Exploring Your Mind, 16 Sept. 2020, exploringyourmind.com/parents-affect-childrens-mental-health/.

27. Scott, Elizabeth. "Coping With Financial Stress in Your Life." Verywell Mind, About, Inc., 26 Mar. 2020, www.verywellmind.com/understanding-and-preventing-financial-stress-3144546.

28. "Genetics and Twins: the TWIN-E Project." Stanford Medicine, Stanford Medicine, 2020, med.stanford.edu/williamslab/research/complete/twins.html.

CHAPTER 4

1. Fisher, Nicole. "Americans Sit More Than Anytime In History And It's Literally Killing Us." Forbes, Forbes Magazine, 7 Mar. 2019, www.forbes.com/sites/nicolefisher/2019/03/06/americans-sit-more-than-anytime-in-history-and-its-literally-killing-us/#3d04de33779d.

2. Michos, Erin Donnelly. "Sitting Disease: How a Sedentary Lifestyle Affects Heart Health." Johns Hopkins Medicine, The Johns Hopkins University, www.hopkinsmedicine.org/health/wellness-and-prevention/sitting-disease-how-a-sedentary-lifestyle-affects-heart-health#:~:text=According to the American Heart, taking a toll on health.

3. Laskowski, Edward R. "What Are the Risks of Sitting Too Much?" Mayo Clinic, Mayo Foundation for Medical Education and Research, 21 Aug. 2020,

www.mayoclinic.org/healthy-lifestyle/adult-health/expert-answers/sitting/faq-20058005.

4. "Obesity and Overweight." World Health Organization, World Health Organization, 1 Apr. 2020, www.who.int/news-room/fact-sheets/detail/obesity-and-overweight.

5. Simon, Gregory E, et al. "Association between Obesity and Psychiatric Disorders in the US Adult Population." Archives of General Psychiatry, U.S. National Library of Medicine, July 2006, www.ncbi.nlm.nih.gov/pmc/articles/PMC1913935/#:~:te xt=Obesity is associated with an,between obesity and mood disorder.

6. "Diet and Mental Health." Mental Health Foundation, Oct. 2018, www.mentalhealth.org.uk/a-to-z/d/diet-and-mental-health.

7. "Diet and Mental Health." Mental Health Foundation, Oct. 2018, www.mentalhealth.org.uk/a-to-z/d/diet-and-mental-health.

8. Van De Walle, Gavin. "What Is Bulking? Steps, Diet and More" Healthline, Healthline Media, 6 Feb. 2020.

9. Selhub, Eva. "Nutritional Psychiatry: Your Brain on Food." Harvard Health Blog, Harvard Health Publishing Blog, 16 Nov. 2015, www.health.harvard.edu/blog/nutritional-psychiatry-your-brain-on-food-201511168626/print/.

10. McIntosh, James. "What Is Serotonin and What Does It Do?" Edited by Debra Rose Wilson, Medical News

Today, MediLexicon International, 2 Feb. 2018,
www.medicalnewstoday.com/articles/232248#:~:text=Se
rotonin is a chemical that,, bowels, and blood platelets.

11. Villines, Zawn. "10 Serotonin Deficiency Symptoms
Everyone Should Look Out For." GoodTherapy,
GoodTherapy, LLC, 25 Feb. 2019,
www.goodtherapy.org/blog/10-serotonin-deficiency-
symptoms-everyone-should-look-out-for-0225197.

12. U.S. Department of Health and Human Services and U.S.
Department of Agriculture. 2015–2020 Dietary
Guidelines for Americans. 8th Edition. December 2015.
Available at
http://health.gov/dietaryguidelines/2015/guidelines/.

13. CBS News. "AAA Study Finds Risks of Drowsy Driving
Comparable to Drunk Driving." CBS News, CBS
Interactive, 6 Dec. 2016, www.cbsnews.com/news/aaa-
study-drowsy-driving-dangers-comparable-to-drunk-
driving/#:~:text=AAA study finds risks of drowsy driving
comparable to drunk driving&text=New research shows
how deadly,who sleep for seven hours.

14. Howe, Neil. "America The Sleep-Deprived." Forbes, Forbes
Magazine, 18 Aug. 2017,
www.forbes.com/sites/neilhowe/2017/08/18/america-
the-sleep-deprived/#6a46f32a1a38.

15. Jones, Jeffrey M. "In U.S., 40% Get Less Than
Recommended Amount of Sleep." Gallup.com, Gallup,
19 Dec. 2013, news.gallup.com/poll/166553/less-
recommended-amount-sleep.aspx.

16. "This Is How Sleep Deprivation Hurts Mental Health." EHE Health | This Is How Sleep Deprivation Hurts Mental Health, EHE, www.ehe.health/blog/sleep-deprivation#:~:text=Sleep Deprivation and Mental Health Risks&text=Experts have found that in,upset to giddy in moments.

17. Epstein, Lawrence J. "Sleep and Mood." Get Sleep, Division of Sleep Medicine at Harvard Medical School, 15 Dec. 2008, healthysleep.med.harvard.edu/need-sleep/whats-in-it-for-you/mood.

18. Cherry, Kendra. "How Does Sleep Affect Mental Health?" Edited by Amy Morin, Verywell Mind, Dotdash, 24 Feb. 2020, www.verywellmind.com/how-sleep-affects-mental-health-4783067.

19. Hirshkowitz, Max, et al. "National Sleep Foundation's Sleep Time Duration Recommendations: Methodology and Results Summary." PubMed.gov, U.S. National Library of Medicine, 8 Jan. 2015, pubmed.ncbi.nlm.nih.gov/29073412/.

20. Cherry, Kendra. "How Does Sleep Affect Mental Health?" Edited by Amy Morin, Verywell Mind, Dotdash, 24 Feb. 2020, www.verywellmind.com/how-sleep-affects-mental-health-4783067.

21. Bhandari, Smitha. "Exercise and Depression." WebMD, WebMD, 18 Feb. 2020, www.webmd.com/depression/guide/exercise-depression.

22. "Physical Health and Mental Health." Mental Health Foundation, 10 Feb. 2020, www.mentalhealth.org.uk/a-to-z/p/physical-health-and-mental-health#:~:text=But when considering mental health, increased risk of some conditions.

23. Bhandari, Smitha. "Exercise and Depression." WebMD, WebMD, 18 Feb. 2020, www.webmd.com/depression/guide/exercise-depression.

24. Bhandari, Smitha. "Exercise and Depression." WebMD, WebMD, 18 Feb. 2020, www.webmd.com/depression/guide/exercise-depression.

CHAPTER 5

1. Childress, Sarah. "A 'Noble Experiment': How Solitary Came to America." PBS, Public Broadcasting Service, 22 Apr. 2014, www.pbs.org/wgbh/frontline/article/a-noble-experiment-how-solitary-came-to-america/.

2. Breslow, Jason M. "What Does Solitary Confinement Do To Your Mind?" PBS, Public Broadcasting Service, 22 Apr. 2014, www.pbs.org/wgbh/frontline/article/what-does-solitary-confinement-do-to-your-mind/.

3. Breslow, Jason M. "What Does Solitary Confinement Do To Your Mind?" PBS, Public Broadcasting Service, 22 Apr.

2014, www.pbs.org/wgbh/frontline/article/what-does-solitary-confinement-do-to-your-mind/.

4. Wykstra, Stephanie. "The Case against Solitary Confinement." Vox, Vox, 17 Apr. 2019, www.vox.com/future-perfect/2019/4/17/18305109/solitary-confinement-prison-criminal-justice-reform.

5. Breslow, Jason M. "What Does Solitary Confinement Do To Your Mind?" PBS, Public Broadcasting Service, 22 Apr. 2014, www.pbs.org/wgbh/frontline/article/what-does-solitary-confinement-do-to-your-mind/.

6. Mental Health Foundation (May 2016) Relationships in the 21st Century. London: Mental Health Foundation

7. Vaillant, G.E. (2012). Triumphs of Experience. The men of the Harvard Grant study. Belknap Press: World.

CHAPTER 6

1. Johnston, Graham. "Preaching to a Postmodern World". Baker Books, 2001.
2. "Shorter Catechism." OPC, The Orthodox Presbyterian Church, www.opc.org/sc.html.
3. Wigglesworth, Smith. "Smith Wigglesworth Quote: 'I Don't Often Spend More than Half an Hour in Prayer at One Time, but I Never Go More than Half an Hour without Praying.'" Quotefancy,

quotefancy.com/quote/908347/Smith-Wigglesworth-I-don-t-often-spend-more-than-half-an-hour-in-prayer-at-one-time-but-I.

CHAPTER 7

1. Leaf, Caroline. "Switch On Your Brain". Baker Books, 2013. Pg. 175, 172
2. Moreland, J.P. "Finding Quiet". Zondervan, 2019. Pg. 67
3. Lawson, Karen. "How Do Thoughts and Emotions Affect Health?" Taking Charge of Your Health & Wellbeing, University of Minnesota, www.takingcharge.csh.umn.edu/how-do-thoughts-and-emotions-affect-health.
4. "Negative Thinking." Rethink Mental Illness., www.rethink.org/advice-and-information/about-mental-illness/learn-more-about-symptoms/negative-thinking.

CHAPTER 8

1. "75 Social Media Sites You Need to Know in 2020." Influencer Marketing Hub, 11 Sept. 2020, influencermarketinghub.com/social-media-sites/.
2. "'Like' It or Not, Social Media's Affecting Your Mental Health." McLean Harvard Medical School Affiliate, McLean Hospital, 26 Feb. 2020,

www.mcleanhospital.org/news/it-or-not-social-medias-affecting-your-mental-health.

3. Migala, Jessica, et al. "'Snapchat Dysmorphia': Is the Stress of Social Media Driving Teens to Plastic Surgery?" EverydayHealth, Everyday Health, Inc., 16 Oct. 2018, www.everydayhealth.com/wellness/united-states-of-stress/what-snapchat-dysmorphia-detailed-look-trend/.

4. Kennedy, Lisa. "A Boulder Filmmaker's New Netflix Documentary Will Make You Want to Delete Social Media Forever." The Know, The Know, 10 Sept. 2020, theknow.denverpost.com/2020/09/10/social-dilemma-netflix-jeff-orlowski/245027/.

5. "How Use of Social Media and Social Comparison Affect Mental Health." Nursing Times, EMAP PUBLISHING LIMITED, 24 Feb. 2020, www.nursingtimes.net/news/mental-health/how-use-of-social-media-and-social-comparison-affect-mental-health-24-02-2020/.

6. Comer, John Mark. "The Ruthless Elimination of Hurry". Waterbrook, 2019. Pg. 40

7. Subrahmanyam K, Kraut RE, Greenfield PM, et al. The impact of home computer use on children's activities and development. The Future of Children/Center for the Future of Children, the David and Lucile Packard Foundation 2000; 10:123–144

8. Hunt, Elle. "Faking It: How Selfie Dysmorphia Is Driving People to Seek Surgery." The Guardian, Guardian News

and Media, 23 Jan. 2019,
www.theguardian.com/lifeandstyle/2019/jan/23/faking-
it-how-selfie-dysmorphia-is-driving-people-to-seek-
surgery.

9. Rogers, Cameren. "'Snapchat Dysmorphia': Seeking Selfie
Perfection." WebMD, WebMD, 10 Aug. 2018,
www.webmd.com/beauty/news/20180810/snapchat-
dysmorphia-seeking-selfie-perfection.

10. Phillips, Katharine A. "Suicidality in Body Dysmorphic
Disorder." Primary Psychiatry, U.S. National Library of
Medicine, 14 Dec. 2007,
www.ncbi.nlm.nih.gov/pmc/articles/PMC2361388/.

11. Susruthi Rajanala, Mayra B. C. Maymone, and Neelam A.
Vashi.JAMA Facial Plastic Surgery.Nov 2018.443-
444.http://doi.org/10.1001/jamafacial.2018.0486

12. "How Use of Social Media and Social Comparison Affect
Mental Health." Nursing Times, EMAP PUBLISHING
LIMITED, 24 Feb. 2020,
www.nursingtimes.net/news/mental-health/how-use-of-
social-media-and-social-comparison-affect-mental-
health-24-02-2020/.

13. Smith A, Anderson M. Social Media Use in 2018 [Internet].
Pew Research Center Internet. Science & Tech. 2018.

14. American Psychological Association. "Mental Health Issues
Increased Significantly in Young Adults over Last
Decade." ScienceDaily, ScienceDaily, 15 Mar. 2019,
www.sciencedaily.com/releases/2019/03/190315110908
.htm.

14. Pantic I, Damjanovic A, Todorovic J, et al. . Association between online social networking and depression in high school students: behavioral physiology viewpoint. Psychiatria Danubina 2012; 24:90–93 [PubMed] [Google Scholar]

15. Kelly Y et al (2018) Social media use and adolescent mental health: findings from the UK millennial cohort study. EClinical Medicine; 6: 59–68.

16. Primak BA et al (2017) Use of multiple social media platforms and symptoms of depression and anxiety: A nationally-representative study among US young adults. Computers in Human Behavior; 69: 1–9.

17. Robinson, Lawrence. "Social Media and Mental Health." HelpGuide.org, HELPGUIDEORG INTERNATIONAL, Sept. 2020, www.helpguide.org/articles/mental-health/social-media-and-mental-health.htm.

CHAPTER 9

1. Muller, Wayne." Sabbath". Bantam Books, 1999. Pg. 8

2. Sword, Rosemary K.M. "Hurry Sickness." Psychology Today, Sussex Publishers, 9 Feb. 2013, www.psychologytoday.com/us/blog/the-time-cure/201302/hurry-sickness.

3. "The Relationship Between Hours Worked and Productivity." Crunch Mode: Programming to the

Extreme - The Relationship Between Hours Worked and Productivity, CS Stanford, cs.stanford.edu/people/eroberts/cs201/projects/crunch mode/econ-hours-productivity.html#:~:text=Thus, overworked employees may simply, in fact, are detrimental).

4. Romano, Andrea. "One Third of U.S. Workers Haven't Taken a Vacation in More Than 2 Years." Travel Leisure, Travel Leisure Group, 3 July 2019, www.travelandleisure.com/travel-tips/travel-trends/third-of-americans-no-vacation-two-years.

5. "American Vacation Deprivation Levels at a Five-Year High." Expedia Brand MediaRoom, Expedia Inc., 16 Oct. 2018, newsroom.expedia.com/2018-10-16-American-vacation-deprivation-levels-at-a-five-year-high.

6. Cline, John. "Are We Really Getting Less Sleep than We Did in 1975?" Psychology Today, Sussex Publishers, 18 Jan. 2010, www.psychologytoday.com/us/blog/sleepless-in-america/201001/are-we-really-getting-less-sleep-we-did-in-1975.

7. Comer, John Mark. "The Ruthless Elimination of Hurry". WaterBrook Books, 2019. Pg.47.

8. Muller, Wayne." Sabbath". Bantam Books, 1999. Pg. 206, 2, 98,18,5

9. Jodi, Clarke. "How the Glorification of Busyness Impacts Our Well-Being." Verywell Mind, Dotdash, 25 June 2019, www.verywellmind.com/how-the-glorification-of-busyness-impacts-our-well-being-4175360

10. Jodi, Clarke. "How the Glorification of Busyness Impacts Our Well-Being." Verywell Mind, Dotdash, 25 June 2019, www.verywellmind.com/how-the-glorification-of-busyness-impacts-our-well-being-4175360

11. Jodi, Clarke. "How the Glorification of Busyness Impacts Our Well-Being." Verywell Mind, Dotdash, 25 June 2019, www.verywellmind.com/how-the-glorification-of-busyness-impacts-our-well-being-4175360

12. Villines, Zawn. "Symptoms of Mental Exhaustion and Tips to Alleviate It." Medical News Today, MediLexicon International, 4 Aug. 2020, www.medicalnewstoday.com/articles/mentally-exhausted#symptoms.

13. Muller, Wayne." Sabbath". Bantam Books, 1999. Pg. 2

14. Muller, Wayne." Sabbath". Bantam Books, 1999. Pg. 98

15. Muller, Wayne." Sabbath". Bantam Books, 1999. Pg. 18,5

16. Angelou, Maya. "Wouldn't Take Nothing for My Journey Now". Random House, 1993

17. Comer, John Mark. "The Ruthless Elimination of Hurry". WaterBrook Books, 2019. Pg.145.

18. Comer, John Mark. "The Ruthless Elimination of Hurry". WaterBrook Books, 2019. Pg.20.

CHAPTER 10

1. Gee, Laura. "Who Was the First Person to Discover Gravity?" Sciencing, Leaf Group Ltd., 30 Apr. 2018, sciencing.com/first-person-discover-gravity-23003.html.
2. Benbow, M. (2010). Birth of a Quotation: Woodrow Wilson and "Like Writing History with Lightning". The Journal of the Gilded Age and Progressive Era, 9(4), 509-533. doi:10.1017/S1537781400004242

Made in the USA
Middletown, DE
04 April 2021